WILL
TRAVEL
FOR BEER

WILL TRAVEL FOR BEER

101 Remarkable Journeys Every Beer Lover Should Experience

STEPHEN BEAUMONT

MITCHELL BEAZLEY

**Dedicated to my all-time favourite travelling companion,
my wonderful wife, Maggie, and all those sympathetic souls
I have encountered on the road.**

An Hachette UK Company
www.hachette.co.uk

First published in Great Britain in 2018 by Mitchell Beazley,
a division of Octopus Publishing Group Ltd
Carmelite House, 50 Victoria Embankment, London EC4Y 0DZ
www.octopusbooks.co.uk
www.octopusbooksusa.com

Text copyright © Stephen Beaumont 2018
Design and layout copyright © Octopus Publishing Group Ltd 2018

Distributed in the US by Hachette Book Group
1290 Avenue of the Americas, 4th and 5th Floors
New York, NY 10104

Distributed in Canada by Canadian Manda Group
664 Annette St., Toronto, Ontario, Canada M6S 2C8

The publishers will be grateful for any information that will assist them in keeping future editions
up to date. Although all reasonable care has been taken in the preparation of this book, neither the
publisher nor the author can accept any liability for any consequences arising from the use thereof,
or of the information contained therein.

Stephen Beaumont asserts the moral right to be identified as the author of this work.

ISBN 978 1 78472 320 0

A CIP catalogue record for this book is available from the British Library.

Printed and bound in China
10 9 8 7 6 5 4 3 2 1

Art Director: Juliette Norsworthy
Designer: Geoff Fennell
Junior Editor: Ella Parsons
Copy Editor: Jamie Ambrose
Picture Research Manager: Giulia Hetherington
Picture Researcher: bluebamboo
Senior Production Controller: Allison Gonsalves

CONTENTS

INTRODUCTION:
WHY TRAVEL FOR BEER?

There are definite advantages to writing about beer for a living. There's the beer, of course: lots of it, if you're doing your job right. There are the people you meet, who number among the most dedicated and yet still relaxed and amiable folk I have ever encountered. And there's the fact that what you do for work – visiting breweries, going to beer festivals, checking out beer bars – most people do just for fun.

Most of all, though, there is the travel.

From the moment I was old enough to comprehend the joy inherent in the discovery of something or some place new, I have been an ardent traveller. In my twenties, I dedicated my first efforts to exploring Canada, the land of my birth; then I ventured into the neighbouring United States, followed by Europe in my mid-thirties. As I grew older still, I journeyed throughout the balance of the world, from São Paulo to Bangkok.

I undertook much of this voyaging hither and thither in the pursuit of great beer, of course – which, as noted above, was and remains a vocation as well as a pleasure for me. For others, however, specifically those not employed in the discovery and evaluation of beer and bars and brewing, a broader issue arises. As my father asked when I first told him about this book: "With so much beer available at home, why would anyone want to travel for it?"

It's a fair question, and one to which I think there are a number of responses.

To begin with, there is discovery. While it is true that today's economy permits the broader distribution of beers previously available in only their home markets, as well as the local re-creation of styles that survived only in small pockets of the world as little as a decade ago, those remain slightly diminished, sometimes even hollow, experiences. Or, at least, that is how they seem when compared with the pleasures of, say, drinking a *gueuze* in a Brussels café alongside a plate of bread, cheese and radishes; enjoying an *altbier* in a Düsseldorf brewery pub; or unearthing a speakeasy-style brewpub in a strictly residential Buenos Aires neighbourhood.

Discoveries like these and many others are where I would

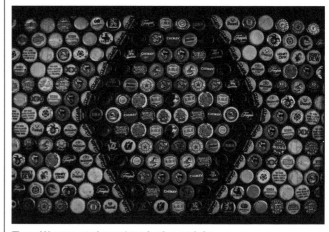

The world boasts greater beer variety today than ever before...

suggest beer lays claim to its true sense of place, and you need to travel to experience them.

Next, there is engagement. In this era of heightened social, cultural and gastronomic awareness, the ability to travel near or far to experience how others live, eat and drink is a glorious opportunity. Since beer is very often the gateway to social understanding – the clichéd but very real "getting to know each other over a beer" – it only makes sense to use a shared interest in ale and lager as a means to making the world a slightly more friendly and understanding place.

Education, of course, figures, in both discovery and engagement, but I think also deserves mention on its own, since the old chestnut about travel broadening the mind remains as valid today as it was when it was first coined. In my travels for beer, I have learned about beer, naturally, but I have also gained knowledge in any number of diverse fields, from religion (while visiting monastic breweries) to cuisine (at beer-focused restaurants and gastronomically inclined brewpubs) to social history (almost everywhere I go).

Lastly, and perhaps most obviously, it's about the beer. Because no matter how great your beer might be at home, I can guarantee that there is even greater beer, almost as great beer or differently great beer being brewed and served almost anywhere you might wish to travel. With the

...but the best places to drink them are still local bars and brewery taps.

expansion of craft brewing now extending to almost every corner of the globe, even the most obscure locales may now yield remarkable beer experiences, a great many of which are detailed on the following pages.

So that's the *why* of travel for beer. In the next section I'll offer a few tips on the *how*, so just before we get started, here are a few words about the *what*.

The 101 beer experiences detailed in this book are culled from my 27 years of covering beer around the world. Most are more recent experiences and all have been thoroughly cross-referenced prior to publication, but there is still a chance that a few of the breweries, bars, restaurants and festivals detailed and recommended will have shut down, changed, been purchased, altered their hours or otherwise undergone significant alteration by the time you read this. Therefore, I strongly

encourage you to double-check the information provided before embarking on your beer travels.

Further, because I haven't been quite everywhere (at least not yet), I have invited a few of my most beer-knowledgeable friends to contribute their experiences to these pages as well. And so, mixed in among my own recollections, you will find essays by my *Best Beers/ Pocket Beer Book* and *World Atlas of Beer* co-author Tim Webb, leading Australian beer writer Matt Kirkegaard and Irish beer-blogging stalwart John "The Beer Nut" Duffy. My profound thanks to each of them for their invaluable contributions.

Now, let's get travelling!

A PRIMER FOR BEER TOURISTS

It is a dedicated beer aficionado who is willing to rise at 6am to line up in the cold for a couple of precious bottles of limited-edition beer. It is an even more committed soul who is up for driving across a state line or two to partake in that same line-up.

Then there are the truly devoted, those who will book vacation time, board a plane, possibly disrupt family schedules and cross oceans for beer. It is for this last class, or rather those who might aspire to join their ranks – my kindred souls, in a way – that this book has been written.

OK, I'M IN.
WHEN DO WE GET STARTED?

The successful beer trip begins weeks, even months, before departure. Because with beer, as with most focused travel, the devil can often lie in the details.

Once you have decided upon your destination, it is imperative to get started with your planning as soon as possible, beginning with your hotel choice. Got a brewery you really want to visit? It might make sense, then, to book a room somewhere nearby or even, as is sometimes the case, adjacent to or above the brewery itself. Want to end your nights at a famous beer bar? Balance the cost of cab fare against the extra you may need to pay for a location convenient to said bar. And it goes without saying that being able to walk back and forth from your hotel to a beer festival is, if not quite priceless, then at least damn close to it.

And about those beer bars, breweries and festivals: research them as well. But bear in mind that the research you should be doing might not be the research you *think* you need to be doing.

The beer rating and "ticking" sites – ratebeer.com, beeradvocate.com and Untappd being chief among them – cover

Beer and food pairing is part of the whole experience.

much more than beers; most also take the measure of bars, pubs, breweries, events... basically anything connected to beer. And while they can be helpful in certain areas, such as addresses and phone numbers, or for scouting out places of genuine mass appeal, they can also grant top rankings to operations with high "wow" factors rather than those of consistent quality, or bestow great praise upon a place that has been coasting on its laurels for perhaps a bit too long.

In particular, when it comes to beer bars, I have found in my experience that raters frequently prize quantities of taps and

bottles over general desirability and hospitality. In other words, simply put, do you want one hundred choices in a grungy sports bar or a few dozen well-selected options in a genuinely convivial locale? For me, it is always the latter.

Fortunately, wherever a beer destination exists these days, there are usually a couple or even several local experts: frequently people with books or blogs coving their patches. In my planning, I regularly look for such individuals – many of whom you will find in the acknowledgements section at the end of this book – always keeping a sharp eye on the date of publication of their latest commentary. I'll even cross-reference their thoughts with those of non-beer specialist travel writers, albeit usually with one eye also on the rating sites.

IT'S TRAVEL TIME:
LET'S GET READY

As much as I appreciate being nimble when I travel, I also like to bring along a few books and bottles to use as thank-yous for people who have helped me out in advance, or who may help me along the way, so relying solely on carry-on luggage is usually a non-starter. My compromise is a lightweight, mid-sized suitcase packed as efficiently as possible. If you're a carry-on-only type, remember that T-shirts and assorted brewery memorabilia can also make appreciated gifts.

While we're on the subject of clothing, my advice is to avoid making brewery and beer-logoed garb your go-to attire. As craft beer becomes more appreciated around the world, as it has long been in traditional beer countries like Belgium, it has increasingly found its way into more upscale restaurants and bars, including many that can provide highly memorable travel experiences. But to get into such places, you will need more than a T-shirt and shorts, so nicer clothes are definitely recommended additions to the wardrobe, especially when travelling around continental Europe and particularly Asia.

Remember, too, that first impressions are also often lasting ones, so if you'd rather not be treated like a stereotypical tourist, it's best not to dress like one. And however unlikely it has become in this day and age, bear in mind that any airline upgrade is going to go to the better-dressed ticket-holder ten times out of ten.

*On a street in Hanoi, barrels of **bia hơì** lie waiting to be transported to local restaurants.*

ON THE GROUND:
GENERAL TIPS AND TRICKS

First off, forget your brewery obsession. Sure, some breweries qualify as definite "must-sees", such as Cantillon in Brussels, Belgium (see page 70); others provide an all-encompassing beer experience, like Spinnakers in Victoria, British Columbia (see page 161). But if it is the beer culture of a city you're after, bars are much more the way to go. Scout out the good ones, talk to the bartenders and servers, connect with the locals. Even if it conflicts with what your research has shown, at least consider following the advice of those you meet. This philosophy has led me to some of the most remarkable places I've visited on my travels, and provided far more after-the-fact stories than have my carefully considered intentions.

The exception to this general brewery rule is the brewery tap, which has become a much more common entity in recent years. In places where such taps proliferate, such as the Bermondsey Beer Mile in London (see page 22), it's not only fun to visit a few, but also useful to research opening days and times so that you can maximize your experience.

In terms of conduct in bars and restaurants, I have found it very beneficial to speak softly and carry a phrase book. The world loves a traveller, but not when that traveller assumes that everyone speaks English, or will if it is spoken more loudly. "Hello," "please" and "thank you" spoken in the local language go a long way toward building harmonious relationships.

In the odds and ends department, I travel with bubble-pack bags for beer cans and bottles, ziplock bags for smelly cheeses and (of course) a bottle opener and a corkscrew.

Finally, and in direct contradiction to some of the advice above, always leave room in your carefully researched itinerary for improvisation. The best travel is a journey, and as much as you might plan and scope and detail that journey, many of its highlights will come from an unexpected twist: a fellow beer fan suggesting a visit to a new bar; an unexpected beer fest recommended by a bartender; a chance brewery discovery; or a "session" spent in a pub not particularly known for its beer cred.

These things have all happened to me and, in many instances, have provided me with my most memorable experiences and most-repeated stories. I'm willing to bet that, if you allow it, one or two will happen to you, too. You'll be delighted they did.

UNITED KINGDOM & IRELAND

THE ORIGINAL
"GREAT" FESTIVAL

Before there was craft beer, before American beer transitioned from punchline to global influencer, and well before beer festivals became the once-a-week occasions they seem to be today, there was the **Great British Beer Festival**.

Founded in 1977 and dedicated to showcasing and promoting British cask-conditioned ale, the GBBF, as it is commonly abbreviated, is the world's oldest continuously running beer festival, one of the largest, and, frankly, still one of the very best. As such, even in a London where hotel costs have skyrocketed, particularly in August when the festival is normally held, it remains an event very much worth the trip.

Over its 40 years, the GBBF has knocked around a bit, going to Birmingham, Brighton and Leeds during the 1980s and shifting from London's Olympia to Earl's Court exhibition centres and back again since returning to the capital for good. And although it is unapologetically cask-ale-focused, it has also matured through the years to include ciders and perries, non-British beers at the Bières sans

For many, the GBBF is a highlight of their social calendar.

Frontières bar and, for the first time in 2017, even British wines. But let's face it: you're at the GBBF for the beer, and unless

ADDRESS BOOK

GREAT BRITISH BEER FESTIVAL
Olympia London, Hammersmith Road, Kensington, London W14 8UX
gbbf.org.uk

you're a dedicated cider fan or a local interested in discovering what's brewing beyond Britain's borders, you're there for cask-conditioned British ale, of which there are hundreds.

Strategy, therefore, is an essential component to making the most of any GBBF experience, beginning with which day or days to choose for your visit. On that front, savvy visitors go early in the week and stay late, thus avoiding the sometimes-chaotic scenes and too-warm ales of Friday and Saturday. On the consumption front, one-third pint measures – as opposed to halves or pints

Above and top: the GBBF at London's Olympia offers a seemingly endless choice.

and milds are best explored earlier in the session, with stouts and strong ales reserved for later in the day.

No matter the day, measure or approach to tasting, though, one thing is almost certain: the GBBF has earned – and very much deserves – its place at the top of the global beer festival hierarchy. It is an event any true beer aficionado should experience at least once in his or her life.

– are best for maximizing the tasting experience.

Next comes a plan for sampling, to prevent the sheer enormity of the fest from overwhelming the senses. Tasting by region can be a fun and interesting experience, since it affords a snapshot of current trends and techniques in, say, Yorkshire or Wales, but proceeding by beer style can be fascinating as well. If choosing the latter, remember that bitters

A NEARLY PERFECT AFTERNOON
AT THE PUB

When I first began visiting Britain for beer in the late 1990s, there was one spot in London that was considered a "can't-miss" destination above all others, the place the late, great beer-writing maven Michael Jackson once described as the finest pub in all of the UK. It was The White Horse on Parsons Green. And although master cellarman Mark Dorber has long since moved on to open a place of his own (see page 26), and the arrival of bars and pubs like those of the Craft Beer Company and Cask Bar and Kitchen have diluted the distinctiveness of the "Sloaney Pony", as it is sometimes called, the pub remains deserving of a stop on any beer traveller's London itinerary. Especially so on a sunny summer's afternoon.

For it is not just the beer that draws people to The White Horse; neither is it just the pub's commendable cuisine, excellent cellarmanship or genial ambience. Instead, while those elements all make the pub stand out among the many public houses that crowd the British capital, what ties it all

The front patio at the White Horse.

together is contained within the pub's extended name: its situation on Parsons Green.

While not particularly expansive, Parsons Green is nonetheless large enough that it provides The White Horse with an enviable setting, whether experienced from inside through the large picture windows that front the pub, or from a table on its just-large-enough outside terrace. Factor in a sunny weekday afternoon when the crowds are at their lightest, a slight breeze blowing off the green and the company of close friends, a loved one or simply a good novel, and you have the makings of what is truly a close-to-ideal afternoon at the pub.

DRINKING IN HISTORY

It will come as no surprise to anyone even vaguely familiar with the city that London is a place of much history. And like any proper city, town or village of note in the United Kingdom, a great deal of that history is contained within its pubs.

It would require an entire book to do any sort of justice to London's sizeable number of historic pubs – a book such as *London Heritage Pubs* by Geoff Brandwood and Jane Jephcote, for instance – so I shall make no such effort here. Instead, to launch you on your own explorations, I shall mention just a few of my personal favourites.

Fans of British writer Pete Brown will be familiar with **The George Inn** of Southwark from the author's *Shakespeare's Local*, or *Shakespeare's Pub* in its North American printing, which details in highly entertaining form the old coaching inn's centuries of life and development. Teeming with history and yet still functioning as a proper pub, The George is structurally reminiscent of what it was like when last rebuilt in 1676 and makes a wonderful contrast to the nearby and quite modern beer bar known as **The Rake**.

Across the River Thames and slightly west lies another visually impressive favourite, **The Blackfriar**, fittingly located near the exit of Blackfriars Underground Station. Recently restored to its full glory, the interior features stained glass, statuary, mosaics and metallic bas-reliefs, all playfully riffing on the monastic theme and all best appreciated during the quieter midweek hours between lunch and dinner.

The Blackfriar

The stunning interior of The Blackfriar.

The George Inn

Ye Olde Cheshire Cheese

ADDRESS BOOK

THE GEORGE INN
75–77 Borough High Street,
London SE1 1NH
george-southwark.co.uk
◆

THE RAKE
Borough Market,
14A Winchester Walk,
London SE1 9AG
utobeer.co.uk/the-rake
◆

THE BLACKFRIAR
174 Queen Victoria Street,
London EC4V 4EG
nicholsonspubs.co.uk/restaurants
◆

YE OLDE CHESHIRE CHEESE
145 Fleet Street,
London EC4A 2BU
◆

THE DOVE
19 Upper Mall, Hammersmith,
London W6 9TA
dovehammersmith.co.uk

While in the area, it would be a shame to miss the nearby **Ye Olde Cheshire Cheese**, a warren of a pub built of stone walls and nooks and crannies. Although the draught beer selection is unlikely to delight, if a mid-afternoon position can be found in the small bar to the right of the entrance, what is in your glass will be almost definitely subjugated by the sense of being transported back to the Victorian era.

The last I shall recommend here is a good distance away, but besides being built most likely in the early to mid-18th century, **The Dove** also happens to be one of the most enchanting pubs in London. The historic part is in the front and certainly deserving of exploration, especially the remarkably tiny snug, while the atmosphere resides in the back, where windows and a modern deck overlook the Thames. History buff or not, there is hardly a better place in West London for whiling away a pleasant spring or summer afternoon.

WALKING THE
BERMONDSEY BEER MILE

You don't need to spend long in beer-forward London spots such as the Cask Pub & Kitchen or the Craft Beer Co. chain before someone will mention the Bermondsey Beer Mile to you. It is the stuff of near-legend in London beer circles, even if its most renowned brewery has decided to shut down its taproom. Before long you may find yourself wondering if you should undertake its completion yourself.

Contemplate no longer. You should.

The first thing to know is that the Mile is not really a mile. In fact, it's closer to two miles, but when you have half a dozen brewery taps to visit, what's a few hundred extra yards between friends? The second important point is that what was once the singular highlight of the Mile for many people is no longer, since the folk behind The Kernel Brewery have decided that they are no longer able to "give our customers an experience, service or environment that we are happy with" and so have shut down their Saturday taproom.

The brewers at Ubrew.

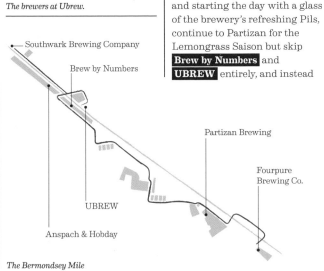

Southwark Brewing Company

Brew by Numbers

Partizan Brewing

Fourpure Brewing Co.

UBREW

Anspach & Hobday

The Bermondsey Mile

Those points understood, the next step is to choose a direction. Assuming that the Mile will be undertaken on a Saturday – that being the only day all six breweries are open – most people will conclude that **Fourpure Brewing Co.** should be the first stop because: a) it will make the earliest-closing **Partizan Brewing** the second stop; and b) the last stop will be relatively close to Bermondsey Underground Station.

The clever Bermondsey Miler, however, will switch things up a bit. Beginning at Fourpure and starting the day with a glass of the brewery's refreshing Pils, continue to Partizan for the Lemongrass Saison but skip **Brew by Numbers** and **UBREW** entirely, and instead

ADDRESS BOOK

FOURPURE BREWING CO.
22 Bermondsey Trading Estate,
Rotherhithe New Road,
London SE16 3LL
fourpure.com

◆

PARTIZAN BREWING
8 Almond Road,
London SE16 3LR
partizanbrewing.co.uk

◆

BREW BY NUMBERS
75 Enid Street,
London SE16 3RA
brewbynumbers.com

◆

UBREW
29 Old Jamaica Business Estate,
24 Old Jamaica Road
London SE16 4AW
ubrew.cc

◆

ANSPACH & HOBDAY
118 Druid Street,
London SE1 2HH
anspachandhobday.com

◆

SOUTHWARK BREWING
COMPANY
46 Druid Street,
London SE1 2EZ
southwarkbrewing.co.uk

Top and above: Fourpure Brewing Co.

venture straight on to **Anspach & Hobday** for its porter and **Southwark Brewing Company** for the London Pale Ale or Gold.

In this fashion, once those last two breweries close, at 6.30pm and 6pm respectively, one can reverse course to Brew by Numbers, which doesn't close until 8pm, and UBREW, open until 11pm, for whatever their ever-evolving line-ups have to offer. Thus, not only is time on the Mile maximized, but its conclusion is reached at the brewery that is closest to the underground station.

It will be a day of good beer and great beer, an almost inevitable disappointment or two, occasionally crowded taprooms, some revelations and a considerable amount of discovery. Or, in other words, a day well spent.

STATION-TO-STATION PUBS

The Sheffield Tap

I love riding the rails in western Europe. From the south of Portugal to the north of Germany, I've had wonderful experiences on clean, fast-moving, mostly on-time trains of all sorts, from the TGV in France to town-to-town clunkers in 1990s Iberia.

Trains in the United Kingdom, however, can be another matter. Like the cobbled-together draught systems I occasionally saw in early North American beer bars, they're great when they work, but are not something you necessarily want to rely upon. Good thing, then, that train-station pubs are beginning to make the entire experience a little more pleasurable.

Arguably the pioneer of this train-station pub revival is **The Sheffield Tap**. Apparently also known as "The Sheffield Trap", due to its ability to cause those availing themselves of its charms to miss train after train, this original "station tap" opened in 2010, after two years of restoration work on the station's former Edwardian Refreshment Room & Dining Rooms. It became an immediate success. Boasting a dozen kegs and 11 cask hand-pulls, The Sheffield Tap styles itself as a "World

The Parcel Yard

Beer Freehouse" and stocks an ever-rotating array of ales and lagers. That, plus its beautifully rehabilitated bar and fixtures, indeed makes it almost alone worth the trip to Sheffield, and apparently – and thankfully – makes it an inspiration to others.

Some such others include the and the , both of the same parentage, and a "spiritual sister" bar, the . Of the three, I can attest that the Euston Tap, located just outside the exit from London's Euston Station, is a particularly difficult place to pass by after disembarking from even a short train ride, much less a lengthy and difficult one.

Elsewhere in London, Fuller's Brewery does a tremendous job with at King's Cross Station, where I have yet to have a pint or plate of food that was anything less than extremely well prepared and presented.

Good station pubs aren't confined to major cities either. If you need ever to stop at

The Head of Steam Huddersfield

 in Wolverhampton, the pub of the same name, once a CAMRA Country Pub of the Year, is right nearby. Further north, off Platform 1 of Huddersfield Station, sits The Head of Steam Huddersfield. As its name suggests, this is part of a small chain, but it is nonetheless charming and thirst-quenching in its listed four-room premises.

They may not keep the trains running on time, but these pubs and others like them sure make the delays a lot more bearable.

THE NEW GUARD IN MANCHESTER

Convention dictates that all the beer festivals of note in the United Kingdom are presented by the Campaign for Real Ale, known to all as CAMRA, or by one of the organization's regional chapters. Convention needs to get to know thee Indy Man Beer Con.

The **Independent Manchester Beer Convention**, as it is officially called, takes place each autumn in the over-a-century-old Victoria Baths, not far from the city centre. In its short existence it has already been dubbed one of England's most important beer events. Even with the pricing concerns that were raised in 2016 – all ⅓ pint samples were sold at £2.50 ($3.30), although bulk token pricing made things a bit less expensive in 2017 – it has found a fast and firm cadre of loyalists, selling out four of its six sessions in 2017 well within two months of the ticket release.

Undoubtedly, a part of the Indy Man Beer Con's success falls to its location in what is, after all, a simply stunning venue, plus the novelty of drinking in a bathing pool. The greatest part of its

ADDRESS BOOK

INDEPENDENT MANCHESTER BEER CONVENTION
Victoria Baths,
Hathersage Road, Manchester
M13 0FE
indymanbeercon.co.uk

popularity, however, is due to its beer selection – which also happens to be precisely where it parts company with CAMRA festivals.

While the equally but differently laudable Great British Beer Festival and GBBF Winter (see pages 14 and 38) each place their focus on British-brewed and cask-conditioned ales, the Indy Man Beer Con throws open its doors to bottled, canned, keg and cask ales and lagers from a wide range of breweries,

Inside the Indy Man Beer Con.

principally hailing from around the UK, but also from the United States, Belgium, Scandinavia and beyond.

In the context of the often impressively high cost of such beers, with even UK craft breweries sometimes charging eye-watering prices for strong and limited-edition brews, suddenly the £7.50 per pint equivalent cost from 2016 doesn't seem that out of line. Factor in the abundant assortment, a chance to sample "limited editions" and beers seldom seen and the worthy-of-a-second-mention opportunity to drink in a Victorian bathing pool, and you begin to understand why the Indy Man Beer Con has become a bold-letter event on the British beer-drinker's calendar.

COASTAL DRINKING IN
SUFFOLK

For the nautically inclined, Southwold, in coastal north Suffolk, has much to offer, such as an active harbour, the Southwold Lifeboat Museum and a working lighthouse. For the rest of us, there is the beer.

Most famously, Southwold is home to **Adnams**, a brewery fast closing on 150 years of age and the producer of such fine cask ales as its Southwold Bitter and Broadside, not to mention the seasonal and quite tasty Tally-Ho Barley Wine, billed as a "traditional dark ale". When in Southwold, to drink anything else is tantamount to sacrilege. The problem is, when beers like

Adnams boasts almost 150 years of history.

Tally-Ho and Broadside are at their best, Southwold is at its worst: that being the cooler, non-beach-y months. Fortunately, the town boasts pubs of such quality that you won't really care what the weather is like outside.

Such as, for example, **The Crown**, a brewery-owned pub about as far from the brewery and its £15 ($20) tour and tutored tasting – which includes a bottle to go – as it is from **The Lord Nelson**, a coastal pub par excellence. Either will satisfy the thirsty traveller, no matter what the season, but the latter is uniquely hospitable when the winds howl in winter.

Across the River Blyth, on the other hand, and reachable via a short ferry ride or a significantly longer drive, resides **The Anchor**, a pub of no small repute that may be Suffolk's finest. Operated by the husband-and-wife team of Sophie and Mark Dorber, the pub combines all that Mark learned while managing things at the famous White Horse on Parsons Green in London (see page 16) with his and Sophie's natural inclinations toward solid hospitality.

As at the Crown, Lord Nelson and riverside **Harbour Inn**, the local beers are emphasized

(see page 16)

ADDRESS BOOK

ADNAMS
Sole Bay Brewery, Southwold
Suffolk IP18 6JW
adnams.co.uk
◆

THE CROWN
90 High Street, Southwold
Suffolk IP18 6DP
thecrownsouthwold.co.uk
◆

THE LORD NELSON
42 East Street, Southwold
Suffolk IP18 6EJ
thelordnelsonsouthwold.co.uk
◆

THE ANCHOR
Main Street, Walberswick
Suffolk IP18 6UA
anchoratwalberswick.com
◆

THE HARBOUR INN
Black Shore, Southwold
Suffolk IP18 6TA
harbourinnsouthwold.co.uk

The Lord Nelson

on tap and on cask. But since you can take the man out of the White Horse but not the White Horse out of the man, The Anchor also features such beers as Cantillon Gueuze, Meantime London Pale Ale and Schneider Weisse, not to mention servers who will be only too happy to suggest which beers (or even wines) might best complement the pub's impressive and generally delicious menu.

None of which is to say that you absolutely *must* cross the river in order to get a decent meal in Southwold, but the savvy traveller is wise to spend time in both Southwold proper and Walberswick.

Southwold in coastal north Suffolk has much to offer.

BEER BY BRISTOL

There are beer cities in the United Kingdom, like Edinburgh and Leeds, that, while offering a comparative wealth of drinking options, might equally and quite effectively be experienced in a single pub or on a solitary lane. And then there is Bristol.

Through the course of the second decade of the 21st century, Bristol has quietly, almost surreptitiously, grown to be one of Britain's top beer destinations. And to get the most of it, you're going to need to wear out some shoe leather.

Oh sure, you could just stick to the centre-of-town King Street, where locals will tell you there is a spot 150m (less than 500ft) away from which it is possible to sample over 500 different varieties of beer. Some of those varieties – indeed, most of them – will be served in the cellar-like **Beer Emporium**, while a slightly more eclectic and meticulously chosen range is available across the street

Small Bar

ADDRESS BOOK

THE BEER EMPORIUM
15 King Street, Bristol
BS1 4EF
thebeeremporium.net

SMALL BAR
31 King Street, Bristol
BS1 4DZ
smallbar.co.uk/bristol

GRAZE BRISTOL
63 Queen Square, Bristol
BS1 4JZ
bathales.com
◆

MOOR BEER COMPANY
Days Road, Bristol
BS2 0QS
moorbeer.co.uk

LEFT HANDED GIANT
BREWING CO.
Units 8–9 Wadehurst Industrial
Park, St Philips Road, Bristol
BS2 0JE
lefthandedgiant.com

THE PORTCULLIS
3 Wellington Terrace,
Clifton Village, Bristol
BS8 4LE
dawkins-ales.co.uk

Small Bar's inviting interior.

at the boundlessly inviting **Small Bar**. But sticking to the "Beermuda Triangle" also means missing out on some true Bristol gems.

Take the around-the-corner **Graze**, for example, a St Austell Brewery tied house that offers what is possibly the city centre's best bet for dining well with beer.

Or the **Moor Beer Company**'s sharp, stylish and unexpectedly edgy brewery tap; the oddly endearing, ramshackle and, as of early 2017, still very much in development brewery tap of the **Left Handed Giant**; and the Clifton neighbourhood's two-storey, Belgian-friendly **Portcullis** and cask-ale-driven,

ADDRESS BOOK

THE VICTORIA
2 Southleigh Road,
Clifton, Bristol
BS8 2BH
dawkins-ales.co.uk

THE OLD BUTCHER'S
57 North Street, Bristol
BS3 1HJ

THE SPOTTED COW
139 North Street, Bristol
BS3 1EZ
thespottedcowbristol.com

HEN & CHICKEN
210 North Street, Bristol
BS3 1JF
henandchicken.com
◆

BRISTOL BEER FACTORY
TAP ROOM
291 North Street, Bristol
BS3 1JP
bristolbeerfactory.co.uk

homey **Victoria**, both pubs under the oversight of area brewer, Dawkins Ales.

Most of all, though, staying north of the River Avon would mean missing out on all the Southside neighbourhood has to offer, which is not inconsiderable. On the paradoxically named North Street, for instance, an 11-minute walk will take you from **The Old Butcher's**, an outlet co-owned by the local hero brewery Wiper and True, to the atmospheric, frequently candle-lit **Spotted Cow** pub, the **Hen & Chicken**, a local brewery-focused pub with an upstairs comedy club, and, finally, to the somewhat spartan, Scandinavian-esque **Bristol Beer Factory Tap Room**.

Except for the Clifton diversion, that's a walk of about 7 km (4 miles) to experience a handful of Bristol's many beer highlights. To visit them all, I'd advise scheduling several days and packing at least a couple of pairs of shoes.

Exploring all that Bristol has to offer will mean crossing several bridges.

A PAIR OF
NEAR-PERFECT PUBS IN LEEDS

Beer-interested visitors to Leeds are spoiled for choice these days. From such near-to-the-train-station gems as the brewery-cum-beer bar Tapped, the tapas-focused Friends of Ham and the outstanding Indian casual Bundobust to destination breweries such as Northern Monk, Kirkstall and North, there is almost no end to the city's libational diversions.

Which is why it might be all the more surprising when I note that the only thing you really need to know about beer in Leeds is contained in an

Above: The bar at Whitelock's. Below: Turk's Head Yard.

unassuming city-centre lane called Turk's Head Yard. In said lane, spanning a modestly signed stretch between Briggate and Trinity Street near the exit of the Trinity Leeds shopping mall, you will find two pubs of shared ownership. Approached from the Briggate side, the first is **Whitelock's Ale House**, a traditionalist's public house if ever there was one, while the second is **The Turk's Head**, as modern as Whitelock's is old-fashioned. Between the two, they afford healthy glimpses of both the past and present, and possibly even the future, of brewing in Leeds in particular and Yorkshire in general.

Start at Whitelock's, over three centuries old and housed in the first building in Leeds to boast electricity. Approaching the tiled bar that runs almost the length of the pub and appears as an artefact of another age, the wise drinker will spurn the temptation of numerous keg-fed draught taps, some of them modern and quite good, and turn instead to the hand-pulls that line much of the bar. While the pride of Yorkshire's disparate breweries would have been on cask-conditioned display here in years past, today the emphasis is much more on local providers. Still, when one is supping in a place as old as this, the temptation is

ADDRESS BOOK

WHITELOCK'S ALE HOUSE
Turk's Head Yard, Leeds
LS1 6HB
whitelocksleeds.com

◆

THE TURK'S HEAD
Turk's Head Yard, Leeds
LS1 6AH
turksheadleeds.co.uk

◆

NORTHERN MONK BREW CO.
The Old Flax Store,
Marshalls Mill, Holbeck
LS11 9YJ
northernmonkbrewco.com

Northern Monk Brew Co.'s taproom.

strong to indulge in a bit of liquid history, such as Theakston's Old Peculier, an old-school ale for a very old-school pub.

Stay for more than a solitary pint and eventually you will need to visit the lavatory, which is as good a reason as any to decamp next door to The Turk's Head, since that's where the bathrooms reside anyway. On the surface this pub is quite different and unabashedly more modern than Whitelock's, but it doesn't take long to begin noticing the visual cues the designers have implemented to connect the two establishments, from the tiles that line the walls to the simple but elegant wooden cabinetry. Where the smaller of the two pubs marks its own territory, however, is through its dozen draught taps, which might feature a local beer such as Wilde Child's Expatriate IPA as easily as it could something from Italy's Lambrate or Sweden's Omnipollo. Old and new, local and imported, comfortable and, well, comfortable in a slightly different way: all you really need for a thoroughly enjoyable evening drinking beer in the gateway to Yorkshire.

BREWERY VISIT

While there are numerous worth-a-visit breweries in and around Leeds, for atmosphere, uniqueness and, of course, beer, my pick would be **Northern Monk Brew Co.**, housed in a listed building and the sort of place you can stop at for a pint and stay for an afternoon and evening.

A MUSEUM AND
A FITTING PUB
FOR AFTERWARD

In 2015, I was delighted to attend the birthday celebration of a good friend in a north London pub. Having arrived directly from the train station, I had my suitcase in tow and thus invited friendly questions from some of the other guests, most of whom I had not previously met.

"So, where have you come from?" someone asked. "Straight from Canada?"

"No," I replied. "I arrived in the UK several days ago and have been spending some time up in Burton upon Trent."

(Long pause.)

"Why?"

To a non-beer aficionado, that response is both understandable and quite typical. For Burton is not a pretty place. It is a Midlands city of minor modern import and largely industrial background which, not withstanding its annual Bloodstock Open Air heavy metal music festival (the UK's largest), has little to recommend it culturally.

Turn your attention to beer, on the other hand, and Burton has culture aplenty. Breweries, too, including one very large operation called Molson Coors (previously Bass), but those abound in modern-day Britain. Places where you can "discover the history, art and fun of brewing", however, are a damn sight more scarce. I speak of **The National Brewery Centre**, a one-of-a-kind in the UK and home to The National Brewery Centre Museum.

Opened in May 2010 on the site of the former Bass Museum, the museum could serve as a template for other such developments, presenting as it does a wealth of information – on both Burton's extensive

The National Brewery Centre Museum

Outside Coopers Tavern.

brewing history and that of Britain in general – in a format as entertaining as it is educational. For those not so historically inclined, the centre also presents frequent special events, including concerts and beer festivals, offers monthly comedy and jazz club nights, and has a quite decent restaurant and pub on site.

The most fitting end to a day at the Brewery Centre comes not at any official offshoot, however, but at the nearby Coopers Tavern. As much a Burton upon Trent institution as any building in town, the Coopers has been around since the 1800s, when it was part of the Bass Brewery, and they still pour pints the way they used to pour samples of Imperial stout for brewery workers: directly from the barrel in the back of the pub. To drink within its confines is to feel an active part of British brewing history, whether gathered with "the regulars" in the back or hidden away in one of its series of nooks and crannies.

The pub is so much a part of the Burton experience that I once wrote the following headline for a story about the city: "So Long As There's a Coopers, There Shall Always Be a Burton". I believe it still.

ALL IN THE FAMILY
IN MASHAM

The Yorkshire town of Masham is home to slightly more than a thousand inhabitants. Which in modern craft-beer terms might make it prime for one small brewery, or perhaps a brewery and a modest beer-focused pub, at best. It may thus come as something of a surprise that Masham is home to not one, but two sizeable breweries, and that each brewery is run by a different branch of the same family.

First came **T&R Theakston**, better known simply as Theakston and run today – but not always – by descendants of the founder, Robert Theakston. That "not always" part is important because when the family decided to exit the brewing business by selling the brewery in the 1980s, it was not a unanimously popular decision. Thus, the black sheep of the Theakston clan, Paul Theakston, decided to set up his own brewery, beginning production in 1992. And he did it within a short walk of the former family firm.

For years, that arrangement suited both parties just fine, with Scottish & Newcastle operating the old Theakston brewery and producing beers

The Theakston brewery

The Black Sheep Brewery

like its classic old ale known as Old Peculier, and the **The Black Sheep Brewery** growing steadily on the back of such ales as Black Sheep Best Bitter and Riggwelter. Eventually, though, S&N stumbled onto harder times, ultimately being divvied up between Carlsberg and Heineken, but not before selling the brewery back to a quartet of Theakstons in 2003.

For travellers, things couldn't have worked out better. With one short deviation from the A1 motorway, visitors arrive at two very hospitable breweries, with the visitor centre at The Black Sheep featuring the punny Bistro & Baa...r, which could easily be termed a gastropub were it in London or Manchester rather than the Yorkshire Dales. The Theakston brewery, on the other hand, boasts the delightfully named Black Bull in Paradise – a tasting room. Both breweries provide brewery tours for under £10 ($13) per person.

If you're set to explore the Dales or just making your way from Burton upon Trent to Edinburgh, as I was when I diverted to Masham, it's a fine place to set up a base or simply while away a few hours.

WARMING UP TO WINTER ALES

Beer and brewing history being the inexact science that it is, we cannot be certain that the idea of a "winter warmer" was invented in the UK. Almost certainly the phrase was coined there, but the notion of a strong ale warming the proverbial cockles is so universal that it's hard to give Britons full credit for this one. The winter ales festival, on the other hand, is likely a British creation.

Born in 1997, the **Great British Beer Festival Winter**, formerly the National Winter Ales Festival, takes place annually in late January or early February. It has a tendency to move around a bit. Founded in Glasgow, it has moved to Manchester, Burton upon Trent, then to Derby. Of late, it has settled in Norwich, the "City of Ale".

This peripatetic nature makes long-term planning difficult, but it is fairly certain that the 2019 festival will be staged in Norwich. (Dates beyond this have not been announced at the time of writing.) And if your beer tastes veer toward old ales, stouts, porters and barley wines, this is definitely a festival to note.

The Fat Cat Brewery Tap

ADDRESS BOOK

GREAT BRITISH BEER FESTIVAL WINTER
The Halls, St Andrews Plain, Norwich NR3 1AU (for 2019)
winter.gbbf.org.uk

◆

THE FAT CAT BREWERY TAP
98–100 Lawson Road, Norwich NR3 4LF
fatcattap.co.uk

Following the same course as the GBBF, the GBBF Winter runs from Tuesday to Saturday; the earlier weekdays being recommended for those who have the advantage of not needing to get up for work. As for what to sample: well, the good news is that the British version of "strong" lags a bit behind that of the rest of the world, so the majority of beers will hover around the 5% alcohol by volume (ABV) mark. There is no bad news.

With one-third measures available and 8–10% ABV beers being the exception rather than the rule, plus pay-as-you-go beer and generally low admission prices, there is little reason not to explore the full range available. Plus, Norwich has become an outstanding beer city, with at least 36 breweries and dozens of decent to excellent pubs, so there are ample ways to occupy one's time outside of the fest.

WHILE YOU'RE THERE
About a 20-minute walk from where the GBBF Winter is held, **The Fat Cat Brewery Tap** is worth the stroll for its abundance of choice, including not just the brewery's own beers, but many guest ales, ciders and perries besides.

STAYING OUT OF
JAIL IN INVERARAY

Most travellers who find themselves in Inveraray will likely be there to see the jail or the castle, the town's two leading tourist draws. To stroll through one or both of those and be on your way, however, would be to miss what in my eyes is Inveraray's prime attraction: **The George Hotel**.

OK, I'm biased. I got engaged at The George after my wife casually mentioned on one of our early dates that it was her favourite pub in Scotland, if not the world. But sentiment aside, there are reasons the place so appealed to her.

Originally built as two separate houses in 1770, the properties were combined into The George just over a century later. Now in its seventh generation of Clark family ownership, it remains an inn as well as a pub and restaurant, which is a good thing because, once experienced, The George can be a tough place to leave.

Low-ceilinged and stone-walled, The George is the sort of pub that puts people at ease the moment they enter – even if they're nervous about popping a certain question!

ADDRESS BOOK

THE GEORGE HOTEL
1 Main Street East, Inveraray, PA32 8TT
thegeorgehotel.co.uk

Like most historic UK pubs, it has numerous sections, with each providing a slightly different atmosphere, so it is possible to have lunch in the brightly windowed conservatory, propose marriage a little later on in "bullshit corner" (true story!) and return later for dinner in a cosy nook of what the proprietors call the "cocktail bar".

All of which will, I promise, bring greater enjoyment than either the castle or jail.

Outside the Inveraray Jail. Overleaf: Scenic Inveraray.

MUSIC AND MALT
– BOTH KINDS – ON ISLAY

The "malt" in the **Islay Festival of Music and Malt**, also known as the Fèis Ìle, is not, one presumes, meant as a reference to the principal ingredient in beer. After all, the modest island off the southwest Scottish coast is home to nine whisky-makers, including the new Ardnahoe Distillery (set to open in 2018), and only one brewery, Islay Ales. That said, however much you love single malts, there comes a point over a ten-day festival when whisky must be put aside in favour of some other libation, and that is where a pint of Black Rock Ale steps up to shine.

The Fèis Ìle has evolved considerably since my wife and I first visited it several years back, but it has grown no less enjoyable, if perhaps a shade more expensive. There is little in the way of pretence on Islay, so events can only get so fancy – which means that whether you are at a £5 dance, a £25 talk and tasting, or a £150 whisky dinner, pomposity is little tolerated and pure pleasure emphasized.

The highlights for many visitors are the distillery open days, which rotate around the island as the festival continues. Each distillery will manage its day its own way; some organize little more than a day-long

ADDRESS BOOK

ISLAY FESTIVAL OF MUSIC AND MALT / FÈIS ÌLE
Isle of Islay
islayfestival.com

◆

ISLAY ALES
Islay House Square, Bridgend, Islay PA44 7NZ
islayales.co.uk

◆

LOCH GORM HOUSE B&B
Bruichladdich, Islay PA49 7UN
lochgormhouse.com

Loch Gorm House B&B

Attractive Islay.

ceilidh, or party, while others schedule a series of special tutored tastings and tours. Still others offer some combination of the two approaches. Almost all, however, make certain that when whisky-palate overload becomes an issue, a bottle or pint will be nearby for refreshment.

If that bottle or pint is for some reason not Islay Ales, the brewery remains open daily throughout the Fèis Île and even hosts its own open day, usually taking pains to make it one of the most musical – and least expensive – days of the entire festival. Being the island's sole brewery, its various ales, including special-edition beers brewed in conjunction with the different distilleries, are also available in numerous pubs and restaurants around the isle.

These may not be the most famous "malts" on the island, or even number among the top eight or nine, but when the smell of saltwater is in the air and you find yourself in need of a short break from the smoky peatiness of an Ardbeg or Laphroaig, there is little better.

WHERE TO STAY

There are several hotels on Islay, but for my money the best accommodation is found at the private Loch Gorm House B&B, with four delightfully appointed and luxurious rooms at surprisingly affordable rates.

THE PICTURE-PERFECT
SCOTTISH PUB

As an inveterate traveller and enthusiastic explorer of beverages, I have likely set foot in hundreds, if not thousands, of bars, taverns, pubs and cafés, scattered throughout dozens or hundreds of cities and towns the world over. The great ones tend to be quite obvious to me. They are the unique places, created not by corporations but by people, each one bearing the distinct imprint of its owner and bestowing special care and attention upon all its varied attributes, from food and drinks to ambience and staffing. One such bar is **The Bow Bar** in Edinburgh.

Found on a narrow street that winds between Grassmarket and the George IV Bridge, the blue-fronted Bow is the sort of place you might pass without noticing if someone hadn't told you about it – or fail to find entirely if you weren't guided there. Once discovered, though, it is a bar that demands your attention – most likely for several hours at a stretch.

Long and thin, with a frontage made up almost entirely of windows, the bar part of The Bow Bar begins about a third of the way back into the room and is lined with hand-pumps and keg taps (more of the former than the latter) all stocked with beers of interest, from local ales to English imports and German lagers and wheat beers. If not familiar with what's on cask, a person can simply pick from the eight on offer and take a chance. I've yet to find myself in possession of a dud.

Besides your pint, you can opt for a dram of single malt, of which The Bow Bar stocks hundreds. There are not as many as some larger and more celebrated whisky destinations, perhaps, but more than enough to keep even the devoted

ADDRESS BOOK

THE BOW BAR
80 West Bow, Edinburgh
EH1 2HH
thebowbar.co.uk

aficionado satisfied. Best of all, though, is that certain something, or rather collection of somethings, that makes a bar or pub great – and the Bow possesses it in spades. Whether it's spending a quiet afternoon seated by the front window, or mixing with the crowds on a Saturday night, the Bow has an unmistakable appeal that goes far beyond the drinks it stocks or the organization of its seating. Something special, something personal, something uniquely its own.

Above and top: The bar and interior at The Bow Bar.

FROM A WEE BAR
TO A LARGER ONE

Early in our relationship, when my Caribbean-born wife first expressed her deep and abiding affection for the city of Glasgow, my surprise was matched only by my scepticism. By then I had travelled a fair bit in Scotland, visiting Edinburgh as well as other, more remote and whisky-centric locales, and never had it so much as crossed my mind to add a stop in working-class Glasgow to my itinerary. Then we visited it together and all my doubts and reservations flew out the window.

By then a veteran of five visits, Maggie was more than adept as a tour guide, showing me the wonderful Kelvingrove Art Gallery and Museum and pointing out the architectural and design work of Charles Rennie Mackintosh as she guided me on our stroll through the city's diverse neighbourhoods. Most importantly, however, she introduced me to Glasgow's pub culture.

While we visited several pubs of interest, including the 200-plus-year-old **Scotia Bar**, which feels as wonderfully old as it is, and **The Pot Still**, the city's premier whisky bar, there were two that stood out for me: **The Wee Bar** and **Tennent's Bar**.

ADDRESS BOOK

THE SCOTIA BAR
112 Stockwell Street, Glasgow
G1 4LW
scotiabar-glasgow.co.uk
◆
THE POT STILL
154 Hope Street, Glasgow
G2 2TH
thepotstill.co.uk
◆
THE WEE BAR AT THE CHIP
12 Ashton Lane, Glasgow
G12 8SJ
ubiquitouschip.co.uk
◆
TENNENT'S BAR
191 Byres Road, Glasgow
G12 8TN
thetennentsbarglasgow.co.uk

The Wee Bar is attached to the Ubiquitous Chip restaurant.

One of a pair of pubs connected to the famous Glasgow restaurant, The Ubiquitous Chip, the Wee Bar is – obviously – the smaller partner to the restaurant's Big Pub and reputedly the tiniest public house in Scotland. That said, it provides plenty of space for a large handful of patrons to stand and drink, whether partaking of draught Furstenberg Pilsner, the house lager for more than 30 years, or one of a small variety of other draughts or bottles, or a single malt.

Not more than a few dozen paces down Byres Road is the contrast to the Wee Pub's cosiness in the form of Tennent's Bar.

Tennent's Bar

Inside Tennent's Bar.

Although named for Scotland's largely forgettable national lager, the Tennent's is no stranger to quality cask-conditioned ale, offering a half-dozen regular casks, plus four rotating guests, in addition to draught and bottled craft beers from across the UK and beyond.

As open and airy as The Wee Bar is dark and cosy, the Tennent's is dominated by its central, horseshoe-shaped bar, but also provides an ample amount of seating around its periphery, some in surprisingly private alcoves. Most impressively, though, just as The Wee Bar somehow manages to be exclusive and welcoming at the same time, the Tennent's can be as low-key and relaxing during the day as it is vibrant and social after nightfall.

SMALL REBELS AND
METROPOLITAN TAPS

I f you arrive in Cardiff by rail, chances are high that you will quickly find yourself on St Mary Street. And if it is after 5pm on a Friday or pretty much any time on a Saturday afternoon or evening, you will equally find yourself wishing to make a quick exit.

The reason for this is that St Mary Street is the main drag for Cardiff nightlife, and that nightlife is something Cardiff regulars embrace with considerable gusto. Fortunately,

there is a left turn several blocks up the road that will not only get you off the main drag, it will also lead you to a pair of Cardiff's finest pubs. The turn is onto Quay Street, and the first stop is **The City Arms** a mere block away.

Although it is a pub in the Brains portfolio – Brains being the 130-plus-year-old, family-owned regional brewery – The City Arms is not bound by that fact. Indeed, aside from the Brains beers that dominate one bank of taps, there is little about the century-old pub that

feels particularly corporate, including the beer selection.

A favourite for savvy city workers and rugby enthusiasts going to or just emerging from the nearby Principality Stadium, The City Arms has a welcoming feel from the moment you enter, even for first-time visitors. You'll find the square-shaped bar only steps ahead and at the end of said bar you'll discover seven casks of guest ales, mostly from smaller Welsh breweries but also the occasional English or Scottish interloper.

The City Arms from below.

ADDRESS BOOK

THE CITY ARMS
10–12 Quay Street, Cardiff
CF10 1EA
sabrain.com
◆
TINY REBEL CARDIFF
25 Westgate Street, Cardiff
CF10 1DD
tinyrebel.co.uk/bars/cardiff

Inside Tiny Rebel.

Outside Tiny Rebel.

Oddly enough, as wonderful as it is, The City Arms isn't even the best pub on the street corner. No, that honour belongs to **Tiny Rebel** – the lone tied house of the fast-growing, fan-favourite Welsh brewery outside its home town of Newport. There is little that is subtle about Tiny Rebel, from its giant sign announcing "Beer & Food", with an arrow pointing to the entrance, to the large L-shaped bar or the cartoon murals that adorn almost every vertical surface. The beer, however, is very good, sometimes surprisingly so – what else can one say about a "marshmallow porter" called Stay Puft that manages to deliver great complexity and flavour?

Sure, there are various other impressive pubs scattered around Cardiff, with Zerodegrees just down the road and a branch of the Bristol beer institution Small Bar (see page 29) on the other side of St Mary, but with such an exemplary duo situated so closely together, there is little incentive to travel further.

DUBLIN,
NO GUINNESS

ny beer-focused trip to Dublin should begin and end at **The Porterhouse**. Founded in 1996 as a brewpub at one end of the notorious Temple Bar nightlife district, The Porterhouse wasn't the first small-scale brewery in Ireland – the now-Molson Coors-owned Franciscan Well and since-departed Biddy Early preceded it, among a select few others – but it was nonetheless a pioneering force in Irish craft beer. For The Porterhouse not only popularized beer-that-isn't-Guinness in the capital, it also gave others the confidence to follow in its footsteps.

And today, beers like the softly roasted Plain Porter, silken Oyster Stout and complex, simply outstanding XXXX Stout are still deservedly considered staples of the Irish pub scene, now brewed off site and poured in pubs across Ireland. As a visitor, then, paying homage only makes sense. But that needn't mean the time between visits must be filled by endless pints of ordinary and – let's face it – now pretty dull mass-market stout. Far from it.

The savvy beer traveller departing The Porterhouse will trace the path of the River Liffey west for a while before turning north toward **L. Mulligan Grocer**, which is not a grocery shop, but rather

ADDRESS BOOK

**THE PORTERHOUSE
TEMPLE BAR**
*16-18 Parliament Street,
Dublin 2*
theporterhouse.ie

◆

L. MULLIGAN GROCER
18 Stoneybatter, Dublin 7
lmulligangrocer1.weebly.com

◆

57 THE HEADLINE
*56–57 Lower Clanbrassil Street,
Dublin 8*
57theheadline.com

◆

BAR RUA
32 Clarendon Street, Dublin 2
barrua.ie

◆

P. MAC'S
*30 Stephen Street Lower,
Dublin 2*

The Porterhouse

A session at The Porterhouse.

a pub specializing in Irish craft beer and whiskeys of all sorts. Still less than a decade old, it also boasts timeworn charm, 24 mostly Irish draughts, including a pair of cask-conditioned house ales, a lengthy international bottled beer list and a kitchen almost as accomplished as the bar.

A somewhat longer hike due south past St Patrick's Cathedral will land you at another Dublin craft beer gem, **57 The Headline**. A proper modern pub lit by large stained-glass windows on two sides, like L. Mulligan it offers two dozen taps – a large number for the Irish capital – and an atmosphere that is half neighbourhood restaurant and half your friend's well-appointed rec room. With tasting trays of up to nine draught beers, it is also the perfect place in which to further your introduction to Ireland's burgeoning new brewery scene.

A 20-minute wander back north will then take you to **Bar Rua**, Irish for "Red Bar", which is smallish even over its two storeys, modern and stylish, and the only bar on this short and by no means exhaustive tour actually to offer Guinness on tap. Mind you, with 14 other beers on draught, occasional special tap takeover events and a Saaz-hopped pilsner from pub-owner Carrig Brewing on tap, there is no reason to resort to the generic black stuff as you watch the world pass by from your intimate booth by the window on the second floor.

YOU MIGHT ALSO LIKE...

Near to Bar Rua is the attractive, if sometimes slightly too trendy, **P. Mac's**, a dim and atmospheric pub carrying an altogether respectable selection of ales and lagers to be supped by candlelight.

Bar Rua

THE
CRAIC
IN CORK
BY JOHN DUFFY

Less than three hours from Dublin is Ireland's second city of Cork. The city has a strong brewing heritage, which, even in the dark days of the 20th century when Guinness dominated Irish beer, saw Cork sustain two large breweries of its own: Murphy & Sons and Beamish & Crawford.

Murphy's and Beamish stouts are still popular in Cork, though both are now made by Heineken at the Murphy Brewery. More recently, however, Cork has taken its place as the crucible of the Irish craft beer revolution, with ten breweries operating in the surrounding county and pubs in the city that are ideal for getting to know them.

Three pubs and a restaurant in town brew their own, the longest-established of which is **Franciscan Well Brewery**, founded on the north bank of the River Lee in 1998. Molson Coors acquired the company in 2013 and has set up a full-scale production facility in the docks, but the pub still brews specials and seasonals, and its spacious beer garden is home to a number of festivals throughout the year.

The Franciscan Well Brewery is now owned by Molson Coors.

Not far across the river, the city's newest brewpub is also the most spectacular. **Rising Sons Brewery** features a dramatically long bar, while looming up behind it are the bright copper vessels of the brewhouse. The specials are always worth checking out, but the highlight of the core range is the refreshing *witbier*, Grainú Ale.

Further out in the Mayfield neighbourhood, though well served by the number 208 bus, **Cotton Ball Brewing Co.** is welcoming, and its stout, Lynch's, is magnificently flavoursome. Back closer to Rising Sons, **Elbow Lane Brew & Smoke House** specializes in grilled meats and fish, all paired with five beers from the very small in-house brewing system.

Finally, and not to be missed, is **The Bierhaus**, a short hop downriver from Franciscan Well, where you'll find 18 ever-rotating taps of carefully selected Irish and international beer as well as a second-to-none selection of Irish gins. If you're lucky, you might catch a tap takeover from one of the country's top brewers, but even if not, there's always something of note available.

No wonder that in this new era of Irish craft beer, Cork locals are rightfully proud of all that they have.

Rising Sons Brewery

ADDRESS BOOK

FRANCISCAN WELL BREWERY
14B North Mall, Cork
franciscanwellbrewery.com
◆

RISING SONS BREWERY
Cornmarket Street, Cork
T12 WK27
risingsonsbrewery.com
◆

COTTON BALL BREWING CO.
18 Old Youghal Road, Mayfield,
Cork T23 AE78
cottonball.ie
◆

ELBOW LANE BREW &
SMOKE HOUSE
4 Oliver Plunkett Street, Cork
elbowlane.ie
◆

THE BIERHAUS
Pope's Quay, Cork
thebierhauscork.com

The Bierhaus

CONTINENTAL
EUROPE

LAZY AFTERNOONS
IN THE
BIERGARTEN

I have no idea why it is, but when the weather turns balmy there is nothing quite so exhilarating as the enjoyment of a glass, pint or litre of beer in the fresh air. And few, if any, people in the world understand this better than Bavarians.

Indeed, drinking outdoors is something that is almost sacred to Germany's most enthusiastic beer imbibers, which is why they have so many places, so many very large places, in which to do it. Welcome to the joys of the *Biergarten*.

Intended as public gathering spots, Bavarian beer gardens are scattered throughout Germany's largest and second-most-populated state, and range in size from corner terraces hardly larger than a typical bar patio to sprawling chunks of parkland with the capacity to seat and serve thousands. And there is likely nowhere in the country (or, indeed, the world) that provides as much choice for outdoor beer drinking as does Munich.

From the sprawling 8,000-seat **Königlicher Hirschgarten**, located a short S-Bahn ride from downtown, to **Zum Flaucher**, a 2,000-person-capacity *Biergarten*

ADDRESS BOOK

**KÖNIGLICHER
HIRSCHGARTEN**
*Hirschgarten 1, 80639 Munich
hirschgarten.com*
◆

ZUM FLAUCHER
*Isarauen 8, 81379 Munich
zumflaucher.de*
◆

CHINESISCHER TURM
*Englischer Garten 3,
80538 Munich
chinaturm.de*
◆

AUGUSTINER KELLER
*Arnulfstrasse 52, 80335 Munich
augustinerkeller.de*

on the banks of the River Isar, to the unexpectedly peaceful, 7,000-seat **Chinesischer Turm** in the centre of the Englischer Garten and (a personal favourite) **Augustiner Keller**, adjacent to the central train station, there seems to be no end to the city's al fresco imbibing opportunities. And while beer selection does tend to be limited, with the beers of only one of the city's six major breweries generally poured, there is equally a *Biergarten* to suit every mood, from fanciful to relaxing to fun with the family.

Visitors are advised to do their homework before they travel, though, for while a half-dozen beer halls might be passed on a central city walk, *Biergärten*, for all their size, still tend to be hidden away – to one side or around the back of a large building, in the middle of a park or in a comparatively obscure part of town. Blink and you just might miss a great one.

Augustiner Keller

THE WORLD'S LARGEST BEER PARTY
ISN'T WHAT YOU THINK IT IS

In stories about Munich's legendary **Oktoberfest**, writers have a nasty yet recurring habit of describing the event as the world's largest beer festival. It is not. There are all of six breweries represented in the big tents at Oktoberfest, four of which are owned by a pair of international brewing companies, Anheuser-Busch InBev (Spaten and Löwenbräu) and Heineken (Hacker-Pschorr and Paulaner). The other two are Hofbräu and Augustiner, the latter being truly independent and the former owned by the Bavarian government. There is wheat beer as well, sold at a special carousel, but that's all Franziskaner, which is also AB InBev-owned.

Not much of a beer festival, then. So why put it in a book about the world's greatest beer destinations? Because sometimes the destination is much more important than the beer. Simply, Oktoberfest is less a beer festival or even a beer party than it is a Bavarian cultural

Each tent at Oktoberfest features one of the "Big Six" Munich breweries.

ADDRESS BOOK

OKTOBERFEST
Munich, Germany
Dates vary, but the event usually runs from mid-September to the first weekend of October.
oktoberfest.de
◆

SCHNEIDER BRÄUHAUS
Tal 7, 80331 Munich
schneider-brauhaus.de
◆

HOFBRÄUHAUS MÜNCHEN
Platzl 9, 80331 Munich
hofbraeuhaus.de

festival. That they have seen fit to invite the world is generous of them and very lucky for us.

Although much of the globe views Oktoberfest as a place where tourists go to get drunk and sway to *oom-pah-pah* versions of "The Chicken Dance" and "Take Me Home, Country Roads", the reality is that traditionally 85 percent of those who attend the event over its 18 days are German, while 82 percent of those Germans are Bavarian, leaving visitors to account for a mere 15 percent.

So, go be part of that 15 percent, but take note of the following Oktoberfest tips before you do:

◆ Book your hotel early. Munich sells out quickly, and if you want to stay locally, you should be booking a minimum of six months in advance.

◆ If you wait too long to secure a room, consider staying in nearby Augsberg, which is an easy train ride away and usually much cheaper at festival time.

Music at Hofbräuhaus.

◆ To avoid the crowds, plan your visits during the day and leave your nights free to explore the unusually empty beer halls.

◆ For night-time visits, make reservations at the tent you most want to visit, as you will not be served unless you have a seat.

◆ Carry cash. It's the best way to buy your beer.

◆ For those unfamiliar with the one-litre *Mass* stein, the best way to grip it is with your palm wrapped around the glass *inside* the handle.

WHILE YOU'RE THERE
Don't let Oktoberfest take up all of your time. Use your stay in Munich as an opportunity to visit terrific and normally quite crowded beer halls such as the Augustiner Keller (see page 56), **Schneider Bräuhaus** (formerly Weisses Bräuhaus) and the unavoidable **Hofbräuhaus**.

Hofbräuhaus

A PICTURE-PERFECT
DAY TRIP
IN BAVARIA

Above: Inside the beer hall at Andechs. Right: Andechs Abbey

On almost any sunny weekend in Munich, an observant visitor will notice significant traffic on the S8 train of the S-Bahn, largely composed of Munich residents carrying baskets of food and bound for Herrsching. Once there, most will either board a bus, hail a taxi or begin a 45–60-minute hike up a nearby hill. Their destination: **Kloster Andechs**. Or, to be more precise, the beer garden at the Andechs monastery brewery.

For, like their Trappist brethren, the monastics at Andechs produce beer on the site of their *Kloster* (abbey). But unlike the monks behind such brands as Chimay and Orval, these Benedictine brothers also operate a restaurant, beer hall and what is truly one of the most picturesque *Biergärten* in all of Bavaria.

As per the law that governs the running of *Biergärten* in Germany, patrons are permitted to bring their own food to Andechs, which explains all of the picnic baskets spotted on the S-Bahn. For visitors who might balk at assembling a meal from the local grocer, however, there is also a cafeteria that sells victuals of all sorts, from roasted chickens

ADDRESS BOOK

**KLOSTER ANDECHS
BRÄUSTÜBERL**
*Bergstrasse 2, 82346 Andechs
andechs.de*

to pork knuckle and freshly baked bread to sausages and *obazda*, a dish that is an irresistible blend of Camembert, butter and spices.

Of course, to wash down your meal there are Andechs beers, and impressive beers they are, too. While much has been written in praise of Andechser Doppelbock Dunkel, a better place to start would be the lusciously dry Spezial Hell or crisp and yeasty Weissbier Hell. After which one might progress through the Weissbier Dunkel, Vollbier Hell and other brands en route to the dark and densely malty *doppelbock*.

But the fine food and across-the-board impressive beers are not the principal factors that draw Munich residents to the abbey. No, that would be its idyllic setting perched atop a hill within sight of the Alps, with a lake on one side and umbrellas and shade trees for comfort when the sun gets too hot. For even with Munich's abundance of lovely *Biergärten*, Andechs truly is special enough to be worth the trip.

SEVERAL BREWERIES, ONE BEER,
PART ONE

Two of the world's finest brewery crawls are located within a half-hour train ride from one another. And each features but a single style of beer.

Style number one is *kölsch*, which is named for city number one, Köln, better known to English speakers as Cologne. Often dismissed as "just another blond beer", *kölsch*'s origins are found in the northward creep of pale lagers that originated in Pilsen, in what is now the Czech Republic, and made their way rapidly across Germany. Faced with such competition, the brewers of Cologne landed

on a style that was pale and cold-conditioned like a lager, but which employed a traditional ale yeast with warm fermentation.

Today, *kölsch* is one of the most tightly regulated beers in the EU, to the point where permitted production areas are defined, filtration is mandatory and producers even have to serve it in a cylindrical, 200ml glass known as a *Stange*. None of which means that there is no variety among its brewers!

Start your tour where all tourists do: outside the city's famous cathedral at the glowing red sign of **Brauhaus Früh am Dom**, where you will commence with a subtly fruity, approachable

kölsch and first experience a service ritual that will be repeated almost everywhere you go. Blue-clad waiters known as *Köbesse* wander the aisles with trays of freshly poured beer, replacing glasses the moment they are empty and marking the sale on a coaster beneath, a cycle that will only stop after you signal the end by placing your coaster atop your glass.

Proceed onward through the stunning Alter Markt, or Old Market, to **Gaffel Haus Köln**, where fruitiness gives way to hoppiness and, while a certain sense of subtlety is lost, a potent source of refreshment is found. From there, a stroll down the

Brauhaus Früh am Dom

A Stange of Früh kölsch.

Brauerei Päffgen

ADDRESS BOOK

BRAUHAUS FRÜH AM DOM
Am Hof 12–18, 50667 Cologne
frueh-am-dom.de
◆

GAFFEL HAUS KÖLN
Alter Markt 20–22, 50667 Cologne
gaffel-haus.de
◆

BRAUEREI ZUR MALZMÜHLE
Heumarkt 6, 50667 Cologne
brauereizurmalzmuehle.de
◆

BRAUEREI PÄFFGEN
Friesenstrasse 64–66,
50670 Cologne
paeffgen-koelsch.de

atmospheric length of the Heumarkt will bring you to **Brauerei zur Malzmühle**, where a slightly rustic maltiness in the beer reflects the farmhouse-style atmosphere of the beer hall.

The next walk will be your longest – a good 25 minutes to the edge of the old city, where **Brauerei Päffgen** resides. Here, seated at long wooden tables and surrounded by locals, the beer you will drink is aromatic and spicy in its hoppiness: the ideal beer with which to end an ideal *kölsch* crawl.

Gaffel Haus Köln

SEVERAL BREWERIES, ONE BEER,
PART TWO

Not far up the Rhine from Cologne is that city's rival, Düsseldorf, home to the other of the world's finest brewery crawls.

Of course, "rival" does not truly describe the relationship between the two cities. If you were to defend the *kölsch* style while in Düsseldorf, almost everyone within earshot would rise to explain how wrong you were, whereas if you were to defend Düsseldorf's *altbier* while in Cologne, the reaction would most likely be a shrug.

Which is to say that Düsseldorf has a rivalry, where Cologne has a superiority complex.

In terms of the attractiveness of the respective city brewery-tap tours, however, they are equals. The difference is that where *kölsch* is golden and pale and served in 200ml glasses, *altbier* is dark and earthy and served in stubbier 250ml glasses.

The walk from the train station to your first destination will take about 20 minutes: long enough to work up a thirst for the drily earthy, very lightly fruity *altbier* of **Hausbrauerei zum Schlüssel**, the "key" (*Schlüssel* means "key") brewery. Schlüssel's open and airy beer hall is in the heart of the Altstadt, or Old City, which has been described as "the world's longest bar", so you know that other stops await.

Tearing yourself away from one *altbier*, then, stroll a few doors up the road to another at **Im Goldenen Kessel**, the in-town tap of the Schumacher brewery. The room feels as much like a restaurant as it does a beer hall, but worry not: they will be just as happy if you partake only of Schumacher's paler, softer and more delicate take on the style, with floral notes and a hint of light fruitiness to its maltiness.

The brewery at Uerige.

Above: inside at Schlüssel. Top: The brewery at Schlüssel.

A five-minute walk (nothing is that far away here) brings you to **Brauerei im Füchschen**, a somewhat darker and, during the day, more moody beer hall that comes alive as the sun goes down. Theirs is the fruitier take on the style, with a less assertive hopping than the others and a round, even slightly creamy maltiness.

Back through the heart of the Altstadt and close to the edge of the Rhine sits what is for many the crowning glory of *altbier* production, **Uerige Obergärige Hausbrauerei**, known phonetically as *Uh-rig-uh* for short. Select from one of six rooms in which to drink and settle in to enjoy what the brewery immodestly but

probably rightly calls the "Alt of the City": a dark, earthy and dryly bitter classic. And then stay for another – at least.

A DOUBLE RENAISSANCE
IN BERLIN

The beer scene in Berlin is quite unlike the beer scene anywhere else in Germany. For one thing, as opposed to Bavarians who sometimes appear amazed to find that beer is brewed outside Bavaria's borders, Berliners tend to welcome imports of all sorts, from Belgian lambics to hoppy American ales – even those produced within the city limits, but more about that later.

Secondly, in contrast to most parts of Germany outside of the capital, the pale lager-dark lager-wheat beer triumvirate

Offerings from Stone Brewing.

does not necessarily rule the city – although this still being Germany, its influence is still most certainly felt. And thirdly, the style of beer most identified with the city, *Berliner weisse*, had

all but vanished from the local market only a few years ago, although it is now making a bit of a comeback.

Let's begin with that last part, since the *Berliner weisse* renaissance is one of Europe's great beer stories. Tangy, low in strength and, even in these beer-adventurous times, a taste that remains challenging for some, *Berliner weisse* was in steep decline before it was embraced by New World brewers interested in revitalizing moribund beer styles. This led to a situation in which there were more and better Berliners in the United States than there were in Berlin.

Inside at Stone Brewing.

The exterior at Stone Brewing.

The front beer garden at the Muted Horn.

ADDRESS BOOK

BRAUMANUFAKTUR
FORSTHAUS TEMPLIN
Templiner Strasse 102,
14473 Potsdam
braumanufaktur.de
◆

STONE BREWING WORLD
BISTRO & GARDENS
Im Marienpark 23, 12107 Berlin
stonebrewing.eu
◆

DAS MEISTERSTÜCK
Hausvogteiplatz 3-4,
10117 Berlin
dasmeisterstueck.de/
berlinmittecraftbeer
◆

MUTED HORN
Flughafenstrasse 49,
12053 Berlin
themutedhorn.com

This is now changing, thanks to brewers such as Schneeeule championing and leading the charge with a complex, *Brettanomyces*-accented Marlene, which can be tough to find but is always worth the search. Also, notable in the revival is **Braumanufaktur**, with a quenching, lemon-zesty *weisse*, reliably available at the brewery in Potsdam, just west of Berlin.

Elsewhere on the Berlin beer scene, the arrival of San Diego's **Stone Brewing**, with its large brewery and restaurant in the city's south, seems to have energized local interest in beer beyond Germany's favourite three styles, even at such popular restaurants as **Das Meisterstück**.

Located in the city centre, Meisterstück complements a menu of toothsome, flame-grilled sausages with eight taps of mostly local small-brewery beers supplemented by Bavarian and occasional international choices. As a retreat from the tourist sites of Mitte, it offers both good value and sufficient selection to slake the thirst of even the most finicky beer aficionado.

For a more international approach, my personal favourite from among the city's growing beer bar circuit is the **Muted Horn**. Located a short walk from the Boddinstrasse U-Bahn stop, the long, very comfortable and somewhat industrial bar delivers a diverse menu of 22 taps that must count among the city's best, complemented by an impressive selection of dozens of bottles –including a healthy array of *Berliner weisse* from across town and around the world.

SMOKE AND HISTORY

The official name of the most famous brewery in Bamberg is Brauerei Heller-Trum, but it is far better known by the name that adorns its tavern and beers: **Schlenkerla**.

Schlenkerla the brewery and Bamberg the city are famous for their smoked malt beers, which in the case of Schlenkerla are very smoky indeed. Most of their beers are brewed entirely from malt that has been smoked over beechwood. This produces forceful flavours that are prized by connoisseurs, but, admittedly are not to everyone's taste. For the more tentative among us, there is **Brauerei Spezial**, a mere 12-minute walk away.

In common with many other *rauchbier* (literally "smoke beer") breweries in the Bavarian subregion of Franconia, the smokiness of Spezial's beers is much more soft and subtle than that of its more famous neighbour. Its *lagerbier* approaches perfection in its balance, while the slightly weightier Rauchbier Märzen can be viewed as a more gentle and nuanced cousin to Schlenkerla's full and forcefully smoky lager of the same style, and nowhere in the world

Schlenkerla

Inside the beer hall at Schlenkerla.

ADDRESS BOOK

SCHLENKERLA
Dominikanerstrasse 6,
96049 Bamberg
schlenkerla.de

BRAUEREI SPEZIAL
Obere Königstrasse 10,
96052 Bamberg
brauerei-spezial.de

FÄSSLA
Obere Königstrasse 19–21,
96052 Bamberg
faessla.de

BRAUEREI KEESMANN
Wunderburg 5, 96050 Bamberg
braugasthoefe.de/gasthoefe

MAHR'S BRÄU
Wunderburg 10, 96050 Bamberg
mahrs.de

KLOSTERBRÄU
Obere Mühlbrücke 1–3,
96049 Bamberg
klosterbraeu.de

BRAUEREI GREIFENKLAU
Laurenziplatz 20,
96049 Bamberg
greifenklau.de

FRÄNKISCHES
BRAUEREIMUSEUM
Michelsberg 10F, 96049 Bamberg
brauereimuseum.de

CAFÉ ABSEITS
Pödeldorfer Strasse 39,
96052 Bamberg
abseits-bamberg.de

Klosterbräu

will they taste better than in Spezial's centuries-old, dark-wood-panelled *Gasthof*.

For those without a taste for smoke, across the street is **Fässla**, another brewery, with two more, **Brauerei Keesmann** and **Mahr's Bräu**, down the road a stretch. **Klosterbräu**, Bamberg's oldest brewery, sits on the other side of the two rivers, **Greifenklau** is a little further on the road south out of town, and the **Fränkisches Brauereimuseum**, or Franconian Brewery Museum, sits back in the centre near the Kloster Michelsberg, providing a bit of between-brewery-visits historical context.

All this in a UNESCO-recognized city centre that would be a compelling visit even if it did not boast one of Germany's most fascinating beer and brewery cultures. Small wonder that in the 40 years since author Michael Jackson introduced the world to *rauchbier* in his *World Guide to Beer*, the place has become a cherished destination among beer enthusiasts.

WHILE YOU'RE THERE...
If brewery-hopping isn't your thing, a fine selection of Franconian beers may be found at **Café Abseits**, including occasional limited-availability specialities brewed at the nearby Weyermann Maltings.

WHERE TO STAY
Modest accommodation is available at both Fässla and Spezial, thus significantly reducing the time it takes to get to your first brewery of the day.

100-YEAR-OLD BREWERY

The headline is misleading. **The Cantillon Brewery** in Brussels is not actually one hundred years old. It was founded in 1900, so as I write these words it is actually nearer 120 years old. But really, it doesn't look a day over a hundred.

On a more serious note, the brewery, located near the Gare du Midi in south-central Brussels, remains almost unchanged since its founding. What's more, it is still family-owned and operated. It is also one of the premier producers of one of the world's most ancient and antiquated forms of beer: lambic.

In brief, lambic is a beer made with roughly one-third or more unmalted wheat, in addition to barley malt, and seasoned with aged hops that add only their preservative effect and no bitterness. What makes the beer truly special, however, is its spontaneous fermentation by wild, airborne yeasts and subsequent aging and blending, so that one- to three-year-old beers are blended in the same fashion as Champagne: bottle-fermented to near-perfect dryness.

Le Poechenellekelder

ADDRESS BOOK

CANTILLON BREWERY
Rue Gheude 56, 1070 Anderlecht, Brussels
cantillon.be
◆
LE POECHENELLEKELDER
Rue du Chêne 5, 1000 Brussels
poechenellekelder.be

This process and the tart results make lambic a bit of an acquired taste, and there is nowhere better to acquire it

than at the Cantillon Brewery. Following your modestly priced, self-guided tour through the fascinating and marvellously musty old brewery, you will be offered a tasting of a beer that bears greater resemblance to dry sparkling wine than it does other beers. You may try that blended beer, known as *gueuze*, or perhaps a cherry-accented *kriek* or raspberry *framboise*, but whichever beer you do choose to sample, you will emerge from your experience a very different beer drinker than you were when you entered. And you'll be grateful and happy for it.

WHILE YOU'RE THERE

Outside of Cantillon, there is no place in Brussels I like to visit more than **Le Poechenellekelder** – a wonderful, puppet-strewn bar beside the Manneken Pis statue, generally (and mercifully) ignored by all but the most astute of visitors.

THE LIMITLESS POSSIBILITIES OF
ANTWERP AT NIGHT

28

ADDRESS BOOK

OUD ARSENAAL
Maria Pijpelincxstraat 4,
2000 Antwerp
dorstvlegel.be
◆

BEERLOVERS BAR
Rotterdamstraat 105,
2060 Antwerp
beerlovers.be
◆

GOLLEM
Suikerrui 28, 2000 Antwerp
gollem.be
◆

DE GROOTE WITTE AREND
Reyndersstraat 18,
2000 Antwerp
degrootewittearend.be
◆

CAFÉ KULMINATOR
Vleminckveld 32, 2000 Antwerp
◆

DOCK'S CAFÉ
Jordaenskaai 7, 2000 Antwerp
docks.be

Travellers who bother to do more than simply change planes in Belgium's Brussels Airport often venture no further than into the capital, or perhaps catch a train to the immensely alluring medieval city of Bruges. And while either place holds myriad charms, especially for the beer aficionado, to limit oneself to either or even both is to miss out on one of the country's finest cities for beer drinking: Antwerp.

An historically important and still active port, Antwerp boasts the advantage of being as walkable as Bruges yet as cosmopolitan as Brussels. Admittedly it has only a pair of breweries at the time of writing, but many others are within easy reach and there are plenty of outstanding beer cafés clustered around the city centre.

Indeed, so diverse and abundant are Antwerp's laudable beer-drinking destinations that compiling a simple list of bars and cafés to visit is anything but a simple task. Any such list in any form, however, would absolutely need to include the **Oud Arsenaal**.

Oud Arsenaal

Den Engel

ADDRESS BOOK

PATERS VAETJE
Blauwmoezelstraat 1,
2000 Antwerp
patersvaetje.be
◆

QUINTEN MATSIJS
Moriaanstraat/Hoofdkerkstraat,
2000 Antwerp
quintenmatsijs.be
◆

CAFÉ DEN ENGEL
Grote Markt 3, 2000 Antwerp
cafedenengel.be
◆

DE VAGANT
Reyndersstraat 25,
2000 Antwerp
devagant.be

An almost-century-old brown café of infinite appeal, the Arsenaal is a near-perfect combination of local haunt, beer-savvy café and relaxed central gathering place. The beer selection isn't as extensive as at some cafés and, as such, beer-obsessives tend to overlook it, but for great beers at a good price in hospitable confines, it cannot be bested.

Travellers arriving by train may be tempted to make their first stop the imposing Bier Central, a large café and restaurant steps from the central station, but they should not. For as impressive as the sheer volume of beers on the menu might seem, a far better option exists just north of the station at the newer and aptly named **Beerlovers Bar**,

where the beers are more interesting, the servers adept and knowledgeable and the space artsy and inviting.

Heading into the Old Town, where the towering cathedral looms as a wanderer's reference point, **Gollem** would serve as a fitting first stop – the first non-Dutch outpost of the small and well-regarded Amsterdam-based chain. An essential second visit, however, should be to the **Groote Witte Arend**, where beer cuisine is studiously and deliciously the focus and the beer list offers more than ample variety.

From there, where next? Perhaps the vintage beers of the **Café Kulminator** or the beer and food pairing prowess of **Dock's Café**? Or the cathedral-side **Paters Vaetje**,

Paters Vaetje

with its people-watching-friendly loft? Maybe, instead, Belgium's oldest continually licensed café, **Quinten Matsijs**, the **Café Den Engel** or, for a change of pace, a beer and genever at **De Vagant**?

In Belgium's endlessly appealing second city, the choices are almost limitless – and all are within easy reach.

Antwerp Cathedral illuminated at night.

THE WORLD'S MOST ROMANTIC
PUB CRAWL

Let's face it: pub crawls are by their nature not terribly romantic pursuits. Usually they involve many people, copious amounts of alcohol and a necessarily dictatorial overlord whose job it is to keep everyone in check and on schedule, none of which is particularly conducive to the wooing of a significant someone.

Then you arrive in the northern Belgian city of Bruges, and all such preconceptions are thrown out the window. For in this spectacularly beautiful medieval city is a collection of bars, cafés and drinking houses so elegant, so perfectly gorgeous, that they practically drip romance. And that is without even mentioning the moody, cobbled streets that separate them, atmospherically lit with a precision that makes one wonder if the town burghers might be more intent on matchmaking than they are urban planning. Here, the final destination is predetermined

Cambrinus

– we'll get to that later – so the immediate question becomes one of where to start, and the answer is **Bruges Beertje**.

One of Belgium's most renowned beer bars, the "Little Bruges Bear" is hardly the most romantic bar in town, particularly on a weekend, but it deserves an early visit simply because it is so good at what it does. So avoid the crowds that will gather later, drink what the bartender or server tells you is good and then move on to **Cambrinus**.

Sometimes described as "pub-like", I'm more inclined to equate Cambrinus to a well-appointed

Bruges Beertje

De Halve Maan

ADDRESS BOOK

BRUGES BEERTJE
Kemelstraat 5, 8000 Bruges
brugsbeertje.be

CAMBRINUS
Philipstockstraat 19, 8000 Bruges
cambrinus.eu

CAFÉ 'T STOKERSHUIS
Langestraat 7, 8000 Bruges
stokershuis.com

DE GARRE
De Garre 1, 8000 Bruges
degarre.be

BROUWERIJ DE HALVE MAAN
Walplein 26, 8000 Bruges
halvemaan.be

and appealing hotel lobby bar. Find a small table somewhere near the back and order from the list of 400 or so bottles, a number of which are 750ml: well suited to sharing. My suggestion would be something strong and malty: perhaps a Sint Bernardus Abt or Abbaye des Rocs.

The next stop won't be found on many beer "must-see" lists, but the **Café 't Stokershuis** is nevertheless an elegant gem of the city. The name means "distiller's house", so it's hardly surprising that the speciality here is Belgian genever, the precursor to modern gin, rather than beer, although this being Belgium there is a more than respectable selection of the latter. Enjoy its tiny confines with whichever drink you prefer and then double back toward the town square.

You may have to hunt a bit to find the alley down which resides the **Café De Garre**, but

the destination is most definitely worth the search, as you will arrive at one of the city's most elegant, intimate and memorable locations. You may have to wait for a table – you won't be served unless seated – but once ensconced, you will find yourself reluctant to depart. Until, that is, the music switches to a progressively louder version of Ravel's "Bolero", which signals closing time every night, and the end of what is perhaps Europe's most romantic pub crawl.

BREWERY VISIT

De Halve Maan might strike some as being a bit too flashy and manicured for a tour, but any wander around a brewery that finishes with a glass of Brugse Zot is a good wander indeed.

A WALK AMONG THE *FOEDERS*

There is a scene in an old Bugs Bunny cartoon in which Bugs makes good his escape from a giant Elmer Fudd, only to screech to a halt in the castle garden, mesmerized by the long rows of massive carrots that surround him. It is exactly how I felt during my first visit to the northern Belgian brewery **Rodenbach**.

At nearly 200 years old, the brewery specializes in the tart and fruity style of beer sometimes termed "Flemish red ale", but is now more often simply lumped into the catch-all category of "sour beers". Rodenbach is a unique operation. In order to develop the complex flavours characteristic of the brewery's most famous brew, Rodenbach Grand Cru, the beer must first spend time in one of the 294 massive wooden tuns, known as *foeders*, which fill the cellar of the brewery.

Walking among these *foeders* was my "Bugs Bunny" moment, with towering vats as old as 150 years to my left and right, each containing up to 65,000 litres (c. 17,200 US gallons) of beer that will mature for as long as two years before being blended into

Foeders *at Rodenbach.*

the brewery's various brands. Not only is the sight of such quantities of maturing beer hugely impressive – although one never can tell how many of the *foeders* are filled and how many are not – a person can't help but be at least a little bit in awe of the patience and blending skills involved in the creation of such a beer, especially in an era when simplistic lagers are sometimes cranked out in as little as two weeks.

Those carefully constructed beers will vary in tartness according to their ratio of sweeter young beer to tangier mature ale, with Rodenbach Classic containing only 25 percent mature beer, Grand Cru

't Walhalla

ADDRESS BOOK

BROUWERIJ RODENBACH
Spanjestraat 133–141,
8800 Roeselare
cheers.rodenbach.be
◆

'T WALHALLA
Zuidstraat 30, 8800 Roeselare
twalhalla.be

having two-thirds of the older beer blended in, and Rodenbach Vintage being an entirely older, more tart ale. Each must be sampled individually in turn, in order to appreciate its unique characteristics, and there is simply nowhere better to do so than in the town where the beer is made.

WHILE YOU'RE THERE

Roeselare is a town with sufficient charms that you might be tempted to make a day or overnight visit rather than a quickie brewery tour. If so, an hour or two at **'t Walhalla**, a café a block south of the Grote Markt, is a strongly recommended diversion.

TRAPPIST BREWERY TAPS

Arguably the most famous, non-massively advertised beers in the world are those of the Trappist abbey breweries. And not just any of the Trappist family – specifically those of the breweries of the six Orders of Cistercians of the Strict Observance that inhabit Belgium.

Today there are Trappist abbeys with breweries in Italy, Austria, the Netherlands and the United States, with more in development, but most of these, save for those of the Onze Lieve Vrouw van Koningshoeven,

better known as La Trappe, are Johnnies-come-lately. For the real Trappist beer fame, one must turn one's gaze to Belgium.

There are six Trappist abbey breweries in Belgium: three in the Flemish north and three in the Wallonian south. Using

their short-form names, they are: Westvleteren, Westmalle and Achel in the north and Chimay, Rochefort and Orval in the south. It behoves me to mention here that Achel is itself a sort of Johnny-come-lately, it having only restarted brewing in 1998 after a cessation dating to before World War I. But that noted, its beer is really quite good.

As Trappist dictates demand that such beer be produced within the monastery walls, there are limited opportunities to tour these abbey breweries. Fortunately, though, most operate or partner with nearby cafés that allow for an in-depth foray into Trappist beers.

Rochefort, makers of such wonderfully dark, malty and strong ales as Rochefort 8 and Rochefort 10, is the only abbey not to have an associated café. Equally singular, Achel, better known as **Achelse Kluis**, is the only one to operate a café within the abbey walls, catering to the bicycling community with lighter, more refreshing beers than are the Trappist norm.

À l'Ange Gardien is the café of Orval, and almost the only place in the world where you can try the lower-strength, abbey-only version of the one magnificent

The monks oversee the brewing at all the Belgian Trappist breweries.

Above: Auberge de Poteaupré. Top and overleaf: The Abbaye de Notre-Dame de Scourmont, source of the Chimay Trappist ales.

ADDRESS BOOK

ACHELSE KLUIS
De Kluis 1, 3930 Hamont-Achel
achelsekluis.org

À L'ANGE GARDIEN
Orval, 6823 Villers-devant-Orval
alangegardien.be
◆

AUBERGE DE POTEAUPRÉ
Rue de Poteaupré 5,
6464 Bourlers
chimay.com
◆

CAFÉ TRAPPISTEN
Antwerpsesteenweg 487,
2390 Westmalle
trappisten.be

IN DE VREDE
Donkerstraat 13,
8640 Westvleteren
indevrede.be

beer the brewery produces. Not far away, the **Auberge de Poteaupré** offers the beers of Chimay in a sampler that includes the beer enjoyed by the brothers, and also sells samplers of the many cheeses and meats produced by the monastery.

To the north, the **Café Trappisten** is the pleasant but not quite exceptional café of the Westmalle Abbey, which serves the local citizenry with fine, rustic fare and the two classic beers the monastery produces. And the crème de la crème might be the **In de Vrede** café at Westvleteren, where the wonderful and rarest of the Trappist beers are available as easily as one might order a pint at the pub down the road.

WHY THERE IS NO SUCH THING AS
BELGIAN-STYLE BEER

Often you will hear non-Belgian brewers and beer drinkers speak of something they call "Belgian-style" beer. If pressed, they might admit that they don't know precisely what exactly makes a beer "Belgian-style", other than the fact the right yeast was used for its fermentation, but most will attest that they certainly know what's "Belgian-style" when they taste it.

Thing is, you very seldom hear Belgian brewers and drinkers talking about "Belgian-style" beer. And you know why? Because such a thing simply does not exist.

If you have trouble believing this, then a trip to the Belgian town of Essen is in order. More specifically, a trip to Essen in December, for what might just be the best of all the very many beer festivals Belgians run throughout the year: the **Kerstbierfestival**.

Run by the Objectieve Bierproevers Essense Regio (Objective Beer-tasters Essen Region), or OBER, this two-day festival seeks to present as many strong, winter and Christmas speciality beers as possible

Avec les Bons Vœux from Brasserie Dupont.

ADDRESS BOOK

KERSTBIERFESTIVAL
Heuvelhal, Kapelstraat 7,
2910 Essen
kerstbierfestival.be

– close to 200 in recent years – and all from Belgium. Visited midday on Saturday or pretty much any time on Sunday to avoid the worst of the crowds (which, frankly, never get too terribly bad anyway), it is a beer event *par excellence*, making up in harmony and conviviality and damn fine beer what it lacks in its sports-arena atmosphere.

It will not take long to make its point about "Belgian-style" beers, either. Sample a Stille Nacht from Dolle Brouwers, an Avec les Bons Vœux from Brasserie Dupont and a Canaster from Glazen Toren and see if you can make a connection among the three. Follow that with a Bush de Noël, Fantôme Hiver and Achouffe Château d'Ychouffe and try again. Continue with – well, you get the point. The "style" that unites these beers is that they are all brewed in Belgium, not that they taste in any way similar, and mere geography simply does not a style make.

It's a lesson worth learning, and an education that's a lot of fun to experience.

SWISS MOUNTAIN BREWERS

Above and top: Brasserie des Franches-Montagnes, or, as it is known today, BFM.

When I first travelled to the brewery now known as **BFM** (then it was the more formal Brasserie des Franches-Montagnes), I took an uncharacteristically delayed train north from Bern through the mountains, wondering as I went exactly what I was getting myself into. By the time I got to my destination station, in those pre-Google-map years, I had little idea of where I was and even less of a notion as to how I'd get back.

Turns out I was not only closer to the French border than I had imagined, but I was also in the neighbourhood of a wild and wonderful – and, frankly, at the time Switzerland's best – brewery. As I was eventually forced to admit, it was a trip very much worth the inconvenience.

As per the above, it's not easy to get to BFM, particularly during the winter months, when mountain road or rail travel can be challenging. Once there, however, this eccentric and iconoclastic brewery can't help but impress. The product of reformed winemaker Jérôme Rebetez, BFM has had from the outset a different approach to brewing, involving wine and other barrels when barrel-aged beer was far from the sexy subject it is today and experimenting early on with spontaneous fermentation. The brewery's eventual flagship beer was even named after the brewery cat, known as Bon Chien, or "good dog."

While the taproom, La Buvette, had not yet opened at the time of my visit, Jérôme was nothing if not the hospitable host – if by "hospitable" you mean someone willing to feed you beer right up to the very moment you need to leave, racing in order to make the last train south. Still, I couldn't help but be impressed then, as I remain today, by the brewery's beers, and so have no problem recommending this, perhaps the most out-of-the-way, brewery visit in the book. Sometimes the most remote and eccentric breweries are also the ones most worth visiting.

ADDRESS BOOK

BRASSERIE BFM
*Chemin des Buissons 8,
2350 Saignelégier
brasseriebfm.ch*

BEER IN THE CITY OF LIGHT

When you think of fine dining in Paris, any of a number of images likely come to mind, from starched white linens and smartly uniformed servers to fine silverware, artfully plated dishes and extensive wine cellars. What you probably don't envision is beer. Then you arrive at **Qui Plume la Lune**, a restaurant in the 11th arrondissement between Place de la Bastille and Place de la République, and all that changes. Because in Chef Jacky Ribault's kitchen, beer matters.

Which is not to say that the Michelin-starred chef is an expert in *la cuisine à la bière* or that he eschews wine in favour of ale and lager. No, it's more that he and his staff appreciate beer's gastronomic lineage and potential better than possibly any other high-end kitchen brigade in the French capital. This appreciation translates into a tight but well-selected menu of beers, and servers skilled in recommending the right ones to pair with a menu that changes on a more-or-less daily basis, depending on what the chef can source from his trusted

Serving beer at La Fine Mousse.

suppliers of organic produce and sustainable farming. In the world of fine dining, Qui Plume la Lune is an anomaly in the way it approaches beer. In the world of Parisian fine dining, it is almost revolutionary.

Not far removed from Ribault's restaurant, physically and philosophically, is **La Fine Mousse**, considered by many to be the leading beer bar and restaurant in the city. Open only

since 2012, La Fine Mousse – the name means, roughly, "The Delicate Foam" – has from the outset been devoted to the promotion of the burgeoning *biéres artisanales* movement in France. At any given time, at least half of the bar's 20 taps feature the best of French brewing, making the bar half of the establishment ideal for French beer discovery, while a bottle list of over a

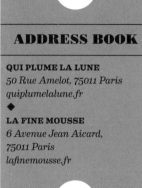

ADDRESS BOOK

QUI PLUME LA LUNE
50 Rue Amelot, 75011 Paris
quiplumelalune.fr
◆
LA FINE MOUSSE
6 Avenue Jean Aicard,
75011 Paris
lafinemousse.fr

hundred selections offers a more global perspective. Over on the restaurant side, ten taps and a gastronomically inclined bottle list complement a kitchen, which, while not quite reaching the culinary heights of Qui Plume la Lune, still demonstrates ably its considerable skill and finesse. Well-trained and educated servers are, again, only too happy to offer advice on beer and food pairings.

Taken together, these fine establishments provide ample evidence of beer's gastronomic prowess, and prove that, even in the wine-drenched City of Light, there are many who appreciate that fact.

La Fine Mousse

35

A NORTHERN
FRENCH
EXPERIENCE

Where France is concerned, I was always more a Provence kind of guy than a Nord-Pas-de-Calais person, despite the latter's importance in the country's brewing history. This was mostly a fact of circumstance, though, because my aunt and uncle lived in Apt for quite some time and I visited them often in my thirties.

Following their deaths, however, I found I had less attraction to the south and grew increasingly interested in the north, visiting Lille and occasionally hopping across the border from west Flanders in Belgium to what is informally known as French Flanders or, more properly, the French *département* of Nord, or North. Still, I wasn't quite convinced of the area's charms until *World Atlas of Beer* co-author Tim Webb insisted one Belgian visit that we drive over for a night in Cassel. Almost immediately, I was hooked.

Built on the upper slopes of Mont Cassel, the town has existed in one way or another for centuries, but feels today like a clever combination of the best of northern France and northern Belgium, with a mix of styles that makes it at once seem very Flemish, then almost immediately and reassuringly French. And at the heart of it all is beer. There are no actual breweries in the town, but for a place that, on the surface, appears to be removed from almost everything, it is actually well placed where beer is concerned.

Not far to the almost immediate north of town is Esquelbecq, home to the iconic French brewery Brasserie Thiriez. South of Cassel, and even closer, is Saint-Sylvestre-Cappel, where can be found the country's top *bière de garde* brewery, Brasserie de St-Sylvestre, better known by its brand name of 3 Monts. Add in everything else that makes the Nord department one of France's better regions for beer and you begin to get a sense of the attraction of Cassel.

It all comes together best at **Kerelshof**, a café on the Grand' Place in the centre of town that some laud as the finest beer bar in all of French Flanders – and with good reason. Although it only offers a handful of beers on tap, the Kerelshof has many more available in bottle and, more importantly, a finger on the pulse of what's going on

Saint-Sylvestre-Cappel

ADDRESS BOOK

KERELSHOF
31 Grand' Place, 59670 Cassel
◆

TRADITIONS EN NORD
36 Grand' Place, 59670 Cassel

Above: Inside at Kerelshof. Top: Kerelshof's exterior.

locally. Arrive in the afternoon, perhaps after a visit to the nearby Musée de Flandres (Museum of Flanders), and you could easily find yourself hanging out, sharing beers with the locals, until well into the night. And the next day you won't be at all sorry that you did.

WHILE YOU'RE THERE
Before departing Cassel, be sure to stop by **Traditions en Nord**, a shop specializing in the foods, spirits and beers of the region, also found on the town's Grand' Place.

A NEST FOR DUTCH BEER
IN AMSTERDAM

Back in 1997, when I first visited Amsterdam, the city's range of good beer discoveries was, to be generous, limited. What the locals called *speciaalbier* – basically anything sold at a premium – was pretty much uniformly Belgian, and beer-specialist cafés were few.

Sure, there were, and still are, **In de Wildeman**, the quintessential Amsterdam beer bar, and Brouwerij 't Ij (see page 90), the then-small, now much larger brewery by the windmill established a couple of years earlier. But apart from those, beer stops were few and far between. For the traveller seeking to sup from a range beyond Heineken and Amstel and Bavaria and Brand, choice in the city was rather severely limited.

Long overshadowed by the brewing fame of Belgium, craft beer in the Netherlands was slow to develop – until at last it did. Beginning with the arrival of the pioneering breweries De Molen and Emilisse, in 2004 and 2005 respectively, breweries have opened at first steadily and then almost exponentially since, to the point that local expert

Outside In de Wildeman.

Tim Skelton estimates that the segment more than quintupled in size between 2002 and 2014. Helping this process along was a very far-sighted restaurateur named Peter van der Arend.

When van der Arend opened the **Arendsnest** on 12 July 2000, it was the first bar in the city, likely the country, to stock exclusively Dutch beer. In fact, he took that mandate one step further by vowing to carry at least one brand from every brewery in the Netherlands – which, of course, meant a lot fewer breweries than today, but it was, he recalls, nonetheless an enormous amount of work.

Accepting that such a goal is today impossible, the Arendsnest still manages to do an excellent job of presenting a remarkable cross-section of modern Dutch beer in a space deserving of the description "elegant". Furthermore, van der Arend is careful to hire and train staff knowledgeable enough to guide visitors through the 30 taps and more than a hundred bottles on offer, thus adding to the appeal for travelling beer enthusiasts.

Frankly, if there is a better place in the world today to explore the full range of brewing in the Netherlands, I cannot say what or where it might be.

WHILE YOU'RE THERE
As wonderful as is the Arendsnest, it would be a shame to visit Amsterdam without dropping in on the grand old man of Dutch beer bars, the aforementioned In de Wildeman.

ADDRESS BOOK

IN DE WILDEMAN
Kolksteeg 3, 1012 PT Amsterdam
indewildeman.nl

ARENDSNEST
Herengracht 90,
1015 BS Amsterdam
arendsnest.nl

Above: The interior at Arendsnest. Top: Arendsnest's streetside patio.

WINDMILLS AND BEER

T o many, the stereotypical symbol of the Netherlands is the windmill. More iconic than tulips, canals or wooden clogs, windmills may still be found across the Dutch countryside, as many as a thousand in number, including all five of the world's largest. Fitting, then, that two windmills figure prominently in the development of craft beer in Holland: one in Amsterdam and the other just over halfway to Rotterdam in the town of Bodegraven.

The first windmill marks the original site of one of the country's earliest and most immediately influential craft breweries, **Bouwerij 't Ij**. Named for the river on which it sits, the brewery's location makes it immediately recognizable and has led to its tasting room being a popular draw for locals and visitors alike since it opened in 1985. Problem is, for much of that time the beers weren't generally all that great. Passable, certainly, even occasionally laudable, but almost never anything to write home about.

That began to change in 2008 when local café owners Bart Obertop and Patrick Hendrikse

Brouwerij 't Ij

bought the brewery from founder Kaspar Peterson and almost immediately began a process aimed at expanding its production and reach, and opening up Amsterdam cafés to beer beyond the ubiquitous golden lager. Soon after, Ij beers, like the long-standing Zatte, a *tripel*, and newer fruity-hoppy session ale Flink, began appearing across the city and, indeed, the country.

Meanwhile, in 2005 Menno Olivier opened his Bodegraven brewery beneath a centuries-old windmill, although by the founder's own admission **De Molen** was not really firing on all cylinders until a year later. Originally brewing beers he believed the citizens of the town would like best, Olivier found instead that the conservative and religious community he was serving wasn't that interested in his beers, and so he stopped making them and instead began brewing beers *he* wanted to drink. Where Ij influenced by its very existence, De Molen's impact was to convince would-be Dutch brewers that there was a market for quirky, oft-changing brews like the brewery's top-selling Op & Top, a hoppy blond ale, and Hel & Verdoemenis, a highly regarded Imperial stout.

Although both breweries have now removed their production from their respective windmills, the original sites remain beacons for beer aficionados, with Ij still running its popular taproom, and De Molen's beers featured at the bar and restaurant beneath the Bodegraven landmark. As with so much in Dutch life, the windmill still marks the spot.

The former De Molen brewery, now the brewery tap and restaurant.

AN ITALIAN IMMERSION

Rimini in the winter months is not much of a draw. Hell, the aging Italian seaside resort town is a destination of questionable merit at any time, quite frankly, but it is indisputably an inhospitable part of the country when the wind blows cold off the Adriatic and the clouds seem never to part. Fortunately, in February, when that winter weather is at its worst, Beer Attraction arrives to brighten up the scene.

Held in conjunction with Italy's national beer competition, Birra dell'Anno, and a trade fair for the brewing industry, Beer Attraction is simply the best place to get a taste of all that is happening in Italian craft brewing. And if you don't find that prospect particularly appealing, well, you haven't been paying attention to Italian beer.

As little as a decade and a half ago, there wasn't much to commend Italian craft beer, aside from a handful of brews from an even smaller number of hallmark breweries, including Baladin, Birrificio Italiano and the now-AB InBev-owned Birra del Borgo. Furthermore, even as brewery numbers rose

precipitously as the first decade of the 21st century gave way to the second, quality remained very much hit and miss in Italy.

Then, as if the entire craft brewing industry experienced a simultaneous epiphany, Italian beer improved dramatically. Pale ales and IPAs, stouts and pilsners, and especially a new category of beers known as "Italian grape ales" suddenly reached levels of interest and character almost unimaginable in the last millennium. It is that last bit that is of particular interest, as Italian brewers have for the most part left behind their youthful fascination with chestnut beers to focus instead

on beers that draw in some way from the country's winemaking traditions, through the use of grape juice, wine lees or simply barrels drawn from wineries. The gastronomically inspired results are, at their best, simply stunning, and even fascinating at their most mundane.

That skill, that flavour, that innovative brilliance is all on display annually at Beer Attraction, and its exploration is more than enough to compensate for the dreadful weather and grey days. Rimini in February may not be a place to associate in any way with the idea of resort or vacation, but in a very short time it has become almost synonymous with great Italian beer.

ADDRESS BOOK

BEER ATTRACTION
Rimini Fiera, Expo Centre, Via Emilia 155, 47922 Rimini beerattraction.it
◆

LA CANTINETTA
Piazzetta Gregorio da Rimini 2, 47921 Rimini cantinettarimini.it

WHILE YOU'RE THERE

When the festival closes for the night, beer enthusiasts head to La Cantinetta, a 200-label beer bar with commendable snack foods and staff savvy enough to guide you through their country's best beers.

Above and top: Beer sampling at Beer Attraction.

PIZZA AND FOOTBALL
AND REALLY GOOD BEER

When I was researching Italian beer in earnest for the first edition of *The Pocket Beer Guide*, I asked Lorenzo Dabove, one of the country's foremost beer authorities, which city I should visit in order to get the best overview of what was happening. Knowing that most of Italy's breweries, and almost all of its best, were then clustered predominantly in the north, I expected his reply might be Milan or perhaps Turin. Instead, he directed me to Rome.

What I did not know but was soon about to learn was that craft beer had become big in the capital – very big, in fact – and that while the breweries might be in the north, the best beer bars were all in Roma, including what might well be *the best*: **Ma 'Che Siete Venuti A Fà**.

Known as simply "the football pub" – to the point that the bar's website is *www.football-pub.com* – the place I've come to know as Ma 'Che Siete is entirely unassuming from the outside, with a simple painted cement exterior and a sign you might easily miss, and a jumbled interior that will probably have

you wondering what all the fuss is about. Fix your gaze more closely, however, and you will find that owner Manuele Colonna has created nothing less than a temple to beer in general and Italian beer in particular.

You won't find a multitude of taps at the football pub, but you will find a selection of draughts and bottles that have been most studiously selected, mostly representative of the best of Italian brewing, but with a handful of European beers included as well. And if the jovial crowding at the front bar

begins to get to you, head toward the back to discover a pub that boasts several comfortable nooks and crannies, plus a lounge area one floor down.

As a bonus, Colonna also operates a restaurant almost across the street that is nearly as good for beer and simply outstanding for pizza. Somewhat more polished than its neighbour, **Bir & Fud** boasts 36 taps and a small selection of outstanding bottles, thus providing a delicious yin to Ma 'Che Siete's uber-casual yang. All this making one section of one street in the Trastevere neighbourhood Beer Central for all of Italy.

The entrance to Ma 'Che Siete Venuti A Fà.

SVĚTLÝ LEŽÁK IN PRAGUE

The beer that most of the world knows as pilsner is not known as such in its home country of the Czech Republic. You see, "pilsner" relates specifically to the town of Pilsen, now Plzeň, so only a beer from there is afforded the designation. Instead, a pale lager with a floral hop character, apparent maltiness and moderate strength is known as a *světlý ležák*, pronounced, more or less, as *svet-lee leh-zhak*.

U Medvídků

While the modern craft-beer world might deride a "pale and fizzy lager", there is a massive difference between mass-market "pilsners" and the balanced and beautiful glory that is a modern or traditional *světlý ležák*. And to learn all about it, there is no better place than the Czech capital of Prague.

OK, maybe that's not quite right. But short of travelling all around the Czech Republic, visiting breweries such as Budějovický Budvar (aka Budweiser Budvar), Kout na Šumavě and Dobruška, pub-crawling in the capital really is the ultimate in *světlý ležák* education. Particularly if it involves places like **U Medvídků**.

While now a brewpub in its own right – the brewing kit is upstairs – U Medvídků earned its early reputation as the best place in Prague for fresh, reasonably priced Budweiser Budvar, known in North America today as Czechvar. The original Budweiser, since its home town was formerly called Budweis and

The Budvar Bar at U Medvídků.

The brewery at U Medvídků.

any beer from there was thus a Budweiser beer, it remains a Czech classic and is best enjoyed in this sprawling beer hall or, weather permitting, in the delightful garden out back.

From a large, old beer hall on one side of the Staré Město, or Old Town, it is only about a 15-minute walk to a small, old beer hall just beyond the other side. That would be **Hostomická Nalévárna**, a taproom for Pivovar Hostomice, taken over by the resurrected brewery not that long ago, but thankfully left mostly unaltered. The Fabian 12° *světlý ležák* demonstrates well how round and floral that style can be.

A longer walk or cab ride across the river to **Na Slamníku** will introduce, in all its floral, bready glory, the Pivo 12° from the Únětický brewery. As a bonus, not only does this pub deliver the homey feel of drinking in an old manor house, it offers both fine Pilsner Urquell as well as the more mainstream-ish Staropramen also on tap.

Světlý ležák 101 now complete, it's back to the old city to continue your education at any of Prague's almost innumerable other fine bars and pubs and beer halls. Because, as we all know, learning is for life!

WHILE YOU'RE THERE

It would be a shame to visit the Czech capital and not drop by the legendary, though admittedly touristy **U Fleků** for its lone beer, the dark Flekovské Ležák, said to be unchanged since it was first brewed in 1843.

U Fleků

THE BEST OF
BARCELONA

There are a multitude of excuses that can be used to justify a trip to Barcelona: tapas, incredible architecture, Spanish cider (*sidra*), Gaudí's Sagrada Familia cathedral, *jamón* in all its many forms. What is not ordinarily used as the basis for such an excursion is beer. Although I suspect that might be shortly about to change. From next to nothing in the way of local brews and places to drink it, Barcelona has blossomed over the past several years into a hub of Spanish craft beer. And a great place to begin any exploration of this largesse is BierCaB.

Every bit a stylish Spanish gathering place that just happens to specialize in beer and food rather than molecular cuisine or Riojas, BierCaB boasts 28 taps that vary between Spanish brews and imports, changing pretty much week to week. To complement is an impressive if slightly pricey menu of beer-friendly Spanish fare, from *hamburguesas* to tapas and, of course, Ibérico ham, true to the bar's slogan of *Cerveza y*

Outside at BierCaB.

Cat Bar

Gastronomía...¿y Porqué No? or, more crudely, "Beer and Food... Why Not?"

From one of the newest to one of the elder statesman beer spots, **Ale&Hop** is a much smaller, more intimate and unapologetically internationalist beer bar and vegetarian restaurant. In between the two in terms of age is the demonstrably popular **La Cerveteca**, a bar that is old school to the core, serving beer, more beer and only beer, once more with a very global tap perspective. Breaking the mould a bit is the quirky, backpacker-ish **Cat Bar**, located not far from the Cerveteca, which provides a most welcome Catalonian approach to beer, along with a vegan menu and a comfortably jumbled décor.

However, for all the appeal of the above quartet, none of them are, in my view and experience, tops in the city for beer. That honour I would give to **Homo Sibaris**. A joyously Spanish beer-focused joint in the Sants district, Homo Sibaris excels in its casual comfort and loyalty to locals, if not sheer volume of beer varieties. In addition to eight taps, all typically serving Catalonian beer, there is a broad selection of domestic and international beers and a fine menu highlighting local cheeses to go with them. Discovered purely by accident, it was a place I had a very tough time convincing myself to leave. I suspect you shall feel the same.

WHILE YOU'RE THERE

A fine excuse for planning a visit is the **Barcelona Beer Festival**, held annually in the spring and a great way to get an overview of the Spanish beer scene in one stop.

Choosing a beer at BierCaB.

THE CHANGING
FACE OF VIENNA

Most brewers and many beer drinkers are easily able to identify the characteristics of the beer most associated with Austria: the Vienna lager. Brewed from a mash that includes lightly toasted Vienna malt – what else? – it has a light amber or bronze hue, a softly sweet maltiness and often a light spice, but finishes dry or off-dry. And up until recently it was seldom if ever found in Vienna.

The great beer scribe Michael Jackson recalled that when he first wrote about the style in his 1977 book, *The World Guide to Beer*, Viennese brewers accused him of having made it up. But Jackson stuck to his guns, insisting that Vienna-brewing notable Anton Dreher invented the style in the mid-1800s as a step toward lighter, more golden lagers, even as his chances of finding one anywhere in Austria at the time were next to none.

The odds are a bit better in Austria today than they were when Jackson last gave voice to his dismay over the disappearance of the style in its native land, and so are the chances of finding a hoppy

1516 Brewing Company

IPA, concentrated *eisbock* or Belgian-inspired strong ale. In fact, chances are high that you'll come across almost any beer style you might care to name.

Always more tolerant of diverse brewing methods and beer styles than their German neighbours, Austria transitioned fully into the multi-beer-style universe with the opening of the **1516 Brewing Company** almost two decades back in Vienna. Innovators from the get-go, the brewery and restaurant early on supplemented its flagship 1516 Lager – a hoppy *helles* rather than a Vienna – with a variety of rotating beers, including Belgian-style wheat beers, or *witbiers*, and, since 2004, its version of Hop Devil

Outside Brauwerk Wien.

The bar at Brauwerk Wien.

IPA, produced in association with Victory Brewing of Pennsylvania.

The much more recently opened and Ottakringer-owned **Brauwerk Wien**, also in Vienna, adopts a similar approach and actually does a splendid job on a cherryish Flanders Red. For (semi-) traditionalists, however, it also offers a Vienna lager, albeit in the form of its 7.2% ABV Imperial Vienna Lager.

Finally, for visitors seeking to explore Austria's brewing industry without leaving their seat, there is **Fassldippler**, a restaurant that prides itself on presenting an overview of the Austrian beer scene through its nine taps and rotating list of 50 or so bottled beers. And in marked contrast to even a decade ago, there is a very good chance of finding a proper Vienna lager beside the IPAs, porters and *märzens* on the menu.

SMOKE AND WHEAT
IN KRAKÓW

Until very recently, the phrase "Polish beer" meant either mass-market lager that was vaguely Czech in character or a frequently misinterpreted and usually underappreciated style known as Baltic porter. Anything else was strictly an anomaly. This situation persisted well into the start of the 21st-century until, as in so many countries around the world, an energetic home-brewing community begat a craft-brewing industry. The way it happened, however, was a little different.

It all began with an ancient style of beer brewed at one time in the city of Grodzisk, a wheat beer brewed with a significant amount of oak-smoked wheat. Said to have been produced since 1301, *grodziskie*, as the beer has since come to be known, was heralded by the late beer scribe Michael Jackson as an "aromatic brew" with a "smoky, dry, crisp palate".

ADDRESS BOOK

MULTI QLTI TAP BAR
Szewska 21, 31-009 Krakow

◆

WEŻŻE KRAFTA
*Dolnych Młynów 10/3,
31-124 Krakow*

◆

OMERTA
Kupa 3, 31-057 Kraków

Multi Qlti Tap Bar

The many beer choices at Multi Qlti Tap Bar.

Those words were enough to spark interest among Polish home brewers, who eventually organized a competition around the style. That contest gave rise to international curiosity, which in turn was enough to spark a small brewery movement, along with, of course, the opening of numerous bars in which to drink the beers these new breweries produced. For these, Kraków wound up being the epicentre. **Multi Qlti Tap Bar** may be the city's best bet for Polish beer, with 20 taps emphasizing local brews alongside a few Czech standards and rotating guest beers from across Europe, all supplemented by a more-than-respectable bottle list. Although centrally located in the old town, seldom does the bar seem over-busy, perhaps owing to its multiple rooms spread over what turns out to be a fairly generous area.

Harder to locate but less than a ten-minute walk from Multi is **Weźże Krafta**, where the tap count is five higher than its near neighbour and the interior much more jumbled. When the weather is nice enough for the patio to be open, however, there may be no better place in the city at which to continue your discovery of all that modern Polish beer has to offer.

Lastly, in the old Jewish district of Kazimierz, the curiously named **Omerta** flies high the flag of Polish craft beer. Decorated in a *Godfather* theme – *omertà* is the Mafia code of silence – each of its two rooms features its own bar with different taps, making it advisable to check both prior to ordering. While you may not find a locally brewed *grodziskie* on tap, you might equally discover a Polish-brewed New England IPA or smoked pepper porter, and return from your visit with a great story to tell.

HUNTING FOLK BEER
IN LITHUANIA
BY TIM WEBB

The decades since Lithuania ceded from Soviet rule in 1990 represent its longest period of independence dating back to the late 15th century. The strength of its cultural identity shines clearly through its desire to mingle with and join others, rather than to exclude them. Is this northern, central or eastern Europe? It depends why you are asking.

The southernmost of the Baltic States is home to a unique set of styles loosely grouped under the heading of *kaimiskas*, or "country beer". Its heartland is the northeastern region of Aukštaitija, otherwise famed for the lakes and

Traditional brewing at Piniavos Alutis.

pine forests of its national park, the strongly accented local dialect and a traditional singing style called *sutartinės*.

Kaimiskas beers are session strength, low in carbonation, murky from lower mashing temperatures and lack of filtration, and earthy from use of homegrown ingredients including wild hops and wilder yeast. Connoisseurs recognize substyles like *šviesusis* (pale), *tamsusis* (dark) and *keptinis* (made from breaded barley), plus unnamed variants that may add hop tea and fresh live yeast, or replace barley with wheat – or, in one case, peas.

For beer and brewing explorers used to testing the limits of ales with high-flavour ingredients, descending into traditional, subsistence-based variations can ironically

The bar at Piniavos Alutis

ADDRESS BOOK

JOVARU ALUS
Alyvu gatvė 2, Jovarai,
LT-83148 Pakruojo

PINIAVOS ALUTIS
Eglyno gatvė 4, Piniava,
LT-38412 Panevėžys
piniavosalutis.lt

SU PUTA
Žemdirbių gatvė 14, Paliūniškis,
LT-38442 Panevėžio

JOALDA
Vytauto gatvė 56, Joniškėlis,
LT-39305 Pasvalio

BAMBALYNĖ
Stiklių gatvė 7, Vilnius 01131
bambalyne.lt

ŠNEKUTIS
Polocko gatvė 7A, Vilnius 01204
jususnekutis.lt

Šnekutis

seem an experiment too far. Travellers seeking tastes from the craft-beer comfort zone should appreciate those from Apynys (from Kaunas), Sakiškių (Vilnius) or craft-trade chameleon Dundulis (Panevėžys). But for a flavour experience to accompany discovering a culture emerging from five centuries of occupation, whether found through museums in fairy-tale castles, the World Heritage coastal ecosystems on the Curonian spit or something plated next to a potato thing, folk beers seem more appropriate.

There are two ways of sourcing *kaimiskas*. The more adventurous will want to plug the street addresses for the **Jovaru**, **Piniavos**, **Su Puta** and/or **Joalda** breweries into their GPS, hope that it recognizes them and further hope that once there, at least one sales counter will be open and staffed by someone who understands a combination of bare-bones English and phrase-book Lithuanian, and has stock.

Method two is easier. Simply drink in or buy from atmospheric cellar bar **Bambalynė** in the Old Town district of Vilnius, then go food pairing with smoked pig's ear and black beans at the Užupis district location of the small **Šnekutis** chain of bars.

Bambalynė

DRINKING
SAHTI
IN A FINNISH SAUNA

This is the most potentially misleading entry in this entire book. Because, frankly, I'm not at all certain what I'm about to describe is even a possibility unless you are a very fortunate visiting beer writer. But in case it is, I very much recommend it. There is also a small fib in the title, but more about that a bit later. First, allow me to explain *sahti*.

Finland's national folk beer, *sahti* is brewed from malted barley supplemented by malted or unmalted rye and sometimes wheat and/or oats. After a lengthy mash, the resulting wort is filtered through juniper boughs, often with fruit attached, and then fermented with a bread yeast, these last processes giving the beer its unique character and flavour. With no hops traditionally used, there is little to preserve *sahti* other than its often significant alcohol content, making it a beer very much meant to be enjoyed *in situ*. Which is where the sauna comes in.

When I was in Finland, I was invited to partake of a "smoke sauna", that being a sauna heated by a wood fire in a stove

A traditional smoke sauna.

ADDRESS BOOK

LAMMIN SAHTI OY SHOP
Tuulonen Shopping Centre,
Tuulosentie 1, 14810 Tuulos; but
you need to find your own sauna.
sahti.fi

with no chimney. Perhaps it was merely the experience of being in the right place at the right time, or maybe it really is my personal preference, but it

is the only sort of sauna I have ever truly enjoyed. Mind you, the beer probably helped, too.

The process went like this: strip down; enter hot sauna; sit and sweat; exit sauna; drink *sahti* from a communal *harrikka* (the classic two-handled, pail-like mug made from juniper wood); repeat. So, the beer was not really enjoyed *in* the sauna, but rather just outside, hence my little fib. After following this order two or three times, I was ready to add a step, that being a quick dip in the nearby lake – entered via a hole cut through its ice cover.

I have enjoyed *sahti* before and since, but never has it tasted as true and delicious as did the Lammin Sahti on that particular day in the middle of Finland's "Sahti Belt", about 125 km (78 miles) north of Helsinki. If the opportunity to do the same ever presents itself to you, I strongly recommend taking it, with a dip in the ice-cold lake purely optional.

ALES AT THE EDGE OF HUMANITY

BY TIM WEBB

At 1:00 am, a watery sun might be high in the sky. The longest day lasts four months, a record matched by the impenetrable night of the Dark Season, when temperatures routinely drop to -20°C (-4°F). Svalbard is a place of practicalities. The first rule handed to visitors in this pristine Arctic environment reads, "Leave nothing behind." The sixth instructs that when leaving the settlements, you must "take a rifle, and the ability to use it". It's the bears.

The most populous place on this icy archipelago 800km (497 miles) off Norway's northern coast is Longyearbyen, which dribbles along the road from the airport to the Miners' Cabins, the quirkiest of its tourist digs. There are no addresses but the bus will go wherever you need. The **Svalbard Bryggeri**, the world's most northerly brewery, half-fills a harbour-side warehouse, just up from the boats that visit the glaciers and the Russian mining communities. Greenpeace's Arctic observation vessel bobs in the inlet beyond them. To its rear are aerial tramways

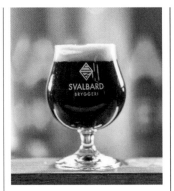

which, until 1987, took coal directly from Norwegian mines to the docks. Skeletons rattling, these form part of a treasure trove of industrial archaeology preserved by the climate.

But for the Russian presence Norway might have quit the islands when its own mines became unprofitable. Instead, they turned to Arctic research and became a year-round destination for extreme tourism. Dark Season visitors zip across ever-replenished virgin drifts on snowmobiles, headlamps dimmed only for a view of the aurora borealis from its polar aspect, in red and blue.

The resident population is international and mostly young, and the beers created here are surprisingly good. A starter pack of 4.7% ABV white, blond and pale ales are clean and serviceable, if unmemorable. The newer

Svalbard Bryggeri

Above and top: Outside and in at Svalbar.

group of 7% ABV offerings – IPA, stout and seasonal brews – are strikingly excellent, cutting it with the best in Tromsø and Oslo. Brewing brilliantly beyond the edge of humankind's natural environment says something of our times – perhaps even of our species.

WHILE YOU'RE THERE

Every hotel and eating place in Longyearbyen serves at least one Svalbard beer, while **Svalbar**, the world's northernmost craft beer bar, stocks 50 others from places to the south.

TWO WEEKENDS OF
DANISH BEER

We live in a world replete with "beer weeks" and you will find but one of them mentioned within these pages, not so much because many have devolved into a seemingly endless series of "meet the brewer" nights, but more due to their sheer ubiquity and resulting loss of specialness. What I can heartily recommend, however, are the two weekends that bookend a week in May and make Copenhagen in the spring the definitive place to be for beer.

It all begins with what was previously known as the Copenhagen Beer Celebration, but has now evolved into the **Mikkeller Beer Celebration Copenhagen**. Presented, quite obviously, by the nomadic brewer turned corporate mogul Mikkel Borg Bjergsø, the celebration highlights international brewers of the Mikkeller school: those who specialize in beers of often unusual style with bold flavours and characters.

As much as Denmark is a nation with a thriving brewing community, to say nothing of the efforts of the neighbouring Scandinavian states, the celebration spreads wide its focus, from Barcelona's Nomada and London's Kernel to Taiwan's Taihu and Creature Comforts of the United States. In total, more than a hundred breweries were represented at the 2017 event, and future editions are almost guaranteed to bring more to the table. For the global explorer of so-called "extreme beers", it presents a cornucopia of possibilities.

On the other hand, the **Danske Ølfestival**, aka the Copenhagen Beer Festival, which occurs the weekend following the celebration, is much more locally focused, welcoming a select group of international brewers but positioning itself

Mikkeller Beer Celebration Copenhagen.

Warpigs

ADDRESS BOOK

**MIKKELLER BEER
CELEBRATION COPENHAGEN**
*Øksnehallen, Halmtorvet 11,
1700 Copenhagen
mikkeller.dk*

◆

**DANSKE ØLFESTIVAL/
COPENHAGEN BEER FESTIVAL**
*Lokomotivværkstedet, Otto
Busses vej 5A, 2450 Copenhagen
beerfestival.dk*

◆

WARPIGS
*Flæsketorvet 25,
1711 Copenhagen
warpigs.dk*

prominently as a showcase for Danish breweries. Which doesn't necessarily tone down the "Oh wow!" factor of the fest, but it does allow for somewhat more studious exploration of flavours.

Ideally, the festivals would be reversed, so that beers like Coisbo's elderflower-accented Urban Haze Pale Ale and Hornbeer's fragrant hybrid brew Dryhop could shine before the big and brawny behemoths arrive the following weekend. But with three days to recover from the celebration before the festival begins on Thursday, and plenty of beery diversions available throughout Copenhagen in between, quibbling about the order in which they appear seems a bit like complaining that perfection could be just a little more perfect.

WHILE YOU'RE THERE

Warpigs, a collaboration brewpub and Texas-style barbecue joint from Mikkeller and Indiana's Three Floyds Brewing, is a highlight on the local beer circuit, if for no other reason than the former slaughterhouse is a great facility and there is almost certain to be at least one beer that pleases among the 22 on tap.

A LITTLE WHISKY
WITH YOUR BEER, PERHAPS

Back when I was just getting started as a beer writer, I had a conversation with Michael Jackson during which I asked the whisky-and-beer-writing maven how and why he had added spirits to his writing repertoire. His response was that, since whisky is, at its core, distilled beer, it simply made sense to him that he extend his coverage to both. Although I have never sought to find out for certain, I suspect that might be the same logic that

the organizers applied to their creation of the **Stockholm Beer & Whisky Festival**.

Entering its 27th year in 2018, the Beer & Whisky Festival spreads itself over two weekends in the autumn, typically with one at the end of September and the other at the start of October. One year I visited, the temptation to combine the first weekend in Stockholm with a few days at Oktoberfest in Munich was too much to resist. It is a travel path I wholeheartedly recommend... For the omnivorous drinker,

there are few if any festivals more appealing.

While the name of this Stockholm event might seem self-explanatory, it really doesn't do itself justice. In addition to offering a very wide range of beers, from not just across Sweden and around its Scandinavian neighbours, but also the US, UK, Canada, Belgium, Japan and well beyond, the festival presents an almost as impressive array of spirits. And not just whiskies and whiskeys – the latter spelling indicative of, mostly, Irish and American

Akkurat

The bar at Oliver Twist.

spirits – but also vodkas, gins, rums and Calvados.

For those interested in award-winners, there are competitions held to award prizes for both beer and spirits, and for tasters wanting to learn more about their favourite beverages, there are tastings and master classes led by experts in their fields.

The brilliance of positioning the festival over six days on two separate weekends means that there is ample time to explore the two halls of the fest. And if you are a truly dedicated visitor, you can reserve one weekend for beer and the other for spirits, taking time in between to explore what is one of northern Europe's prettiest cities.

WHILE YOU'RE THERE

It would be criminal to visit Stockholm and not partake of its two finest beer destinations, **Oliver Twist** and **Akkurat**, located within a stone's throw of each other. While the former is the city's finest beer pub, the latter is a beer-focused restaurant without compare in the country.

ON THE *RUNTUR*

FOR GOOD BEER

49

When planning my first visit to Reykjavik, my online research revealed a local phenomenon known as the *runtur*. Loosely translated to "pub crawl", the *runtur* was a Reykjavik institution, I read, as revered among Icelanders as the midnight stroll down Las Ramblas was to Barcelonans or the "six o'clock swill" was to Australians prior to 1967.

Like the Aussie ritual, which involved the downing of drinks prior to a mandated 6pm bar closing for dinnertime, the *runtur* was a remnant of another era, when alcohol consumption was much more state-controlled than it is today. But unlike the swill, the essence of the *runtur* had prevailed, as I discovered during my 2008 trip.

Beer of above 2% ABV was still illegal in Iceland until 1989, so the country was understandably a little backward when it came to drinking. Spirits had been legal since 1934 and industrious Icelanders had developed the habit of lacing their weak beer with a shot of vodka or the local *brennevin*, resulting in a

Skúli Craft Bar

A small beer at Mikkeller & Friends.

Mikkeller & Friends

ADDRESS BOOK

MICRO BAR
Vesturgata 2, 101 Reykjavík

SKÚLI CRAFT BAR
Fógetagarður, Aðalstræti 9,
101 Reykjavík

MIKKELLER & FRIENDS
Hverfisgata 12, 101 Reykjavík
mikkeller.dk/mikkeller-friends-
reykjavik/

seriously casual relationship with weekend drunkenness. This attitude was deeply ingrained in the Saturday night *runtur*.

Thankfully, much has changed since those days. The country's economic recovery has lessened the impact of European stag parties on the local nightlife, and the advancement of the Icelandic beer palate has resulted in both impressive local breweries and interesting places in which to consume their wares.

Although evocative of nothing so much as a cool friend's basement, **Micro Bar** is arguably the top spot in town for beer, with 14 taps devoted mainly to Icelandic beers (pay particular heed to Ölvisholt and Borg). Given Iceland's re-emergence as a pricey place to visit, the bar's sampler boards of five or ten beers are a great way to assess the local market.

A short walk away is the **Skúli Craft Bar**, a somewhat more harmonious locale with a modern Icelandic aesthetic and a patio on the square for when weather permits. Beer-knowledgeable staff are more than happy to guide visitors through the mixed 14 taps, with a generous selection of local brews and samplers for those who seek exploration.

For those with a more international bent, there is **Mikkeller & Friends Reykjavik**, where the focus is upon – surprise! – Mikkeller beers and those of the brewery's friends, such as fellow Danes To Øl and their Copenhagen offshoot, BRUS. Fine, if you like that sort of thing, but really, did you travel all the way to Reykjavik to drink Danish beer?

THE UNITED STATES OF AMERICA & CANADA

THE SECOND
"GREAT"
FESTIVAL

The world's largest beer festival in terms of available samples is the **Great American Beer Festival** (GABF), an annual autumnal event held in Denver, Colorado. For many dedicated beer fans, both within and without the United States, it is also a pilgrimage of almost sacred reverence.

Regularly offering more than 3,800 beers and welcoming in excess of 60,000 attendees, the GABF has developed near-mythic status over the course of its 35 years and sold out of tickets in just over an hour in 2016. For those who make the trek to Denver and fork out for

a hotel room on what is now one of the city's most expensive weekends, however, the realities of the festival can prove, well, rather sobering.

Perhaps the first surprise is the ticket scalpers plying the sidewalks around the Denver Convention Center: not a

common sight at most beer festivals but typical of the GABF for at least the last decade. Then there are the crowds, which snake in lines outside the Center long before the doors open and jam the interior once let loose inside – although that latter issue has been mitigated somewhat in recent years by the addition of extra square footage.

Most surprising for those who have not done their homework, however, is the minuteness of the samples offered, which are strictly limited to a mere 30ml (1oz) per beer. While this does allow for the visiting of a large number of the 780 or more breweries attending, it can be frustrating when trying to get a handle on the aroma and flavour of, say, a relatively subtle pilsner or *kölsch* or pale ale.

Still, none of those are obstacles that can't be at least somewhat overcome with a little careful planning. To begin with, choose your session wisely. Of the four, Friday and Saturday nights are without question both the busiest and the wildest, while Thursday night is slightly less frenetic, and the relatively laid-back American Homebrewers Association (AHA) members-only Saturday

Great American Beer Festival

Beer served with a smile at the Great American Beer Festival.

afternoon session presents a good case for joining the AHA even if you've never brewed in your life.

Next, plan a strategy and be prepared to deviate from it. In other words, know the breweries you want to visit and the beers you want to taste, but also pay heed to what others on the floor are praising and, if necessary, change your approach so that you might partake of an otherwise unheralded gem. And finally, roam the peripheries of the hall as much as possible. The biggest crowds collect in the centre, so it can expedite your tasting experience if you pursue a strategy of attack and retreat, making a beeline for the brewery table of your desires and then retreating to the fringes after a beer or three.

WHILE YOU'RE THERE

The GABF is now less a festival than a weeklong collection of beer events spread throughout Denver. Visit the venerable **Falling Rock Tap House** early, grab lunch at **Euclid Hall** and find some time to drop by the ever-impressive **Crooked Stave Artisan Beer Project**, but most of all keep your ears open for news of exclusive brewery events.

Falling Rock Tap House

HOP-HARVESTING
IN YAKIMA

In order for you to understand why it's worth travelling to Yakima, Washington, in the fall, you need to first understand the nature of the hop. (Those of you well acquainted with hops and their cultivation can skip ahead.) The spice that gives beer not only its bitterness but, particularly in the new world of hop-forward ales, often a considerable amount of its flavour, hops were originally introduced to brewing for their preservative effect. Most famously, they were enshrined into brewing law via the German beer purity law of 1516 known as the *Reinheitsegebot*, which mandated using only malted barley, hops and water in brewing. Other malted grains and yeast were added later, the latter because it would be some centuries yet before its function was fully understood.

A most voracious vine, the hop plant can grow 7.6m (25ft) or more in a single summer, with farmers sometimes reporting that at the peak of the growing season it is actually possible to watch the growth of the vine. Only female plants are cultivated, to prevent the males from fertilizing the hop cone – the part of the plant prized by brewers. To keep them controlled, they are typically guided along a system of trellises. And they are aromatic. Oh, how they are aromatic!

The compound of the hop responsible for all this aroma and flavour and bittering, and the preservative nature of the plant, is lupulin, a sticky yellow substance found at the core of the hop cone. When agitated, as during the harvest of acre after acre of vines, it gives off a powerful fragrance, and when dried in a kiln, as is standard procedure for hops, that aroma grows even more concentrated and powerful.

And that is the main reason to come to Yakima during harvest time. As the largest hop-growing region in the United States, second in the world to only Hallertau, Germany, the entire valley becomes an olfactory experience during the harvest, with different hops yielding different scents and clashing and combining to create new, airborne aromas. At night, you'll be jostling at the bar with brewers and brewery owners from all over, who are in town to select their hops, but daytime is a chance to sit back, relax and take some time to smell the hops.

ADDRESS BOOK

HOP-HARVESTING IN YAKIMA
For information on visiting during the hop harvest or at any other time, contact Yakima Valley Tourism at visityakima.com.

Harvesting the hops in Yakima.

A BRIEF WALK
IN BEERVANA

There are few cities in the world able to present the palette of brewery options that is available seven days a week in the place they call "Beervana", otherwise known as Portland, Oregon. Mention a style of beer and there is almost certainly a brewery in town specializing in it; try to pin down the exact number of breweries in town and three more will have opened by the time you complete your count.

That said, the sheer size of the Rose City's beer scene and its sprawling nature – more than 26km (16 miles) between Occidental Brewing and Zoiglhaus, and that's without straying from within the city limits – can be frustrating for the visitor seeking to take full advantage of Portland's beery largesse. It is fortunate, then, that there exists a near-perfect trio of city-centre breweries providing a remarkable range of excellent ales and lagers within a short walk of each other.

Although it might seem counter-intuitive, the best place to begin this mini-brewery crawl is in the middle, specifically the new location of San Diego's Modern Times. Formerly the Commons Brewery, the new owners have renamed it **Belmont Fermentorium**. At the time of writing, the new brewery's offerings were still being ironed out, but it's a pretty safe bet that you can count on Fortunate Islands, a delightfully citrusy hoppy wheat ale – an ideal first-beer-of-the-day. Continue

Cascade Brewing Barrel House

Sampling the beer at Hair of the Dog Brewing Company.

with a few of the brewery's other offerings, taking care not to pass on the highly impressive Pils, before heading south to **Hair of the Dog Brewing Company**.

Formerly housed in a rather inhospitable industrial locale, Hair of the Dog has thrived since moving to beside the railway tracks near the Morrison Bridge, offering now not just its rightly lauded strong ales, but also a full menu for diners. Which is good, because food is to be recommended when sipping glasses of culinarily influenced beers such as Fred, a deftly executed strong golden ale with a Belgian accent; the well-hopped but not outrageously bitter double-IPA Blue Dot; and the brewery's flagship ale, Adam, a potent and complex beer worthy of serious contemplation. Be sure to sample whatever has recently been fermented in the special concrete egg fermenter – trust me on this – before returning north to the **Cascade Brewing Barrel House**.

The Cascade specializes in that particular cluster of ales known collectively as "sour beers", although that description does little justice to the multifaceted creations that emerge from the many racks of barrels housed behind the tasting-room wall. Expect tart mixtures of fruit and beer, the latter fermented separately, then long-matured with the fruit in wine barrels of varying pedigrees, most vintage-dated. The brewery's Kriek, a blend with cherries, is Cascade's most notorious creation, but visitors are advised to sample whatever the bartender suggests is new and exciting.

TO GO
For beer to take away with you, visit **Belmont Station**, by some margin the best bottle shop in the central Portland area. As a bonus, it now also boasts a multi-tap bar that stands it in good stead with the best of the Portland taphouses.

BREWING IN WINE COUNTRY

Mention to the average imbiber that Sonoma County, California, is principally a brewing district and they would think you mad. After Napa, they would inform you, Sonoma County is northern California's most important winemaking region, and beer has absolutely nothing to do with it. They would be wrong.

Not about the vinification, mind you – there were actually more acres of wine grapes planted in Sonoma in 2016 than there were in Napa, although the latter has the better reputation – but about

the role of beer. For nowhere does the old adage of it taking a lot of beer to make a great wine ring so true as in Sonoma.

Having spent a lot of time over the course of my career

with wine professionals, wine authors and sommeliers and winemakers alike, I have witnessed firsthand that most enjoy nothing more at the end of their workday than, in a favourite phrase of my Master Sommelier friend John Szabo, "a cleansing pint of ale". Add in the long days of sweaty labour during the harvest and you can double that sentiment.

Which may to a degree explain the early success of the **Bear Republic Brewing Company**, a brewpub in Healdsburg in the centre of Sonoma. Established in 1995 by two generations of the Norgroves, a long-established Sonoma family, the brewery has from its earliest years seen enthusiastic patronage from area winery workers, and has

Above and top: Bear Republic Brewing

Russian River Brewing

ADDRESS BOOK

BEAR REPUBLIC BREWING COMPANY
345 Healdsburg Avenue, Healdsburg, CA 95448
bearrepublic.com/brewpub/
◆
RUSSIAN RIVER BREWING COMPANY
725 4th Street, Santa Rosa, CA 95404
russianriverbrewing.com

grown to the point of opening a full production brewery in Cloverdale, about 26km (16 miles) up the highway.

The expansion takes nothing away from the original pub, however. It is precisely how you would expect a bar in an agricultural region to appear: rustic and roadhouse-ish, although you might not expect the bicycles hanging from the ceiling. A pint or two of the wonderfully quaffable flagship Racer 5 IPA underlines the place's relaxed appeal.

Slightly south of Bear Republic, a brewery actually born of a winery holds forth as perhaps

the most significant in northern California, and for good reason. The **Russian River Brewing Company** was originally part of the Korbel wine family before head office decided to pull the plug on the beer side. They did grant brewer Vinnie Cilurzo and his wife, Natalie, rights to the name, however, and so the duo set up a pub in Santa Rosa and began producing beers the likes of which were unknown to most of the world.

While hundreds flock to Russian River every year for the release of the potent and pale "triple IPA" called Pliny the Younger, the original double IPA – Pliny the Elder – is available at the atmospheric pub year-round, as are such renowned mixed-fermentation beers as the Pinot Noir-barrel-conditioned Supplication and the spontaneously fermented Beatification.

None of these are, admittedly, the sort of beer you would knock back at the end of a hot and sweaty workday, but nonetheless they are exceptional ales worth the wander off the wine-country route.

SUPPING IN THE
CITY BY THE BAY

My first trip to San Francisco was in 1986, as an aspiring music and culture writer. While I toured the city extensively on foot, and no doubt visited numerous bars, I don't recall many of them and I certainly don't remember sampling any great beers.

My next visit, only a few years later, was a much more notable beer trip. I spent a memorable evening at the long-since-closed Twenty Tank Brewpub, visited Anchor Brewing for the first time and somehow found my way to the classic San Francisco beer bar, the **Toronado**. In truth, I'm a bit hazy on the details surrounding this early visit, but I know for certain that I liked the place immensely and envied San Francisco its existence. As I turned my attention increasingly toward good beer over the following years, I recognized in retrospect that the Toronado is, indeed, a very special place.

I have been to the City by the Bay many times since then, almost too often to count, and pretty much every time I have paid a visit to this temple of great beer. It's hardly a stylish place

Above and below: Toronado

– it's on the lower Haight, for crying out loud, where standards aren't exactly high. But while it might not be the most attractive bar in the world, with its low lighting, worn fixtures and furnishings, and low-rent décor, there is a certain something that makes the Toronado one of the great bars on the US West Coast.

Simply put, with its attitude, 45-plus taps and extensive bottle list, Toronado just feels like the consummate place for beer. The walls display it, the floor smells of it and the general atmosphere practically oozes it. You don't go there for wine or spirits or

ADDRESS BOOK

TORONADO
547 Haight Street,
San Francisco, CA 94117
toronado.com

◆

MAGNOLIA GASTROPUB &
BREWERY
1398 Haight Street,
San Francisco, CA 94117
magnoliabrewing.com

◆

THE MONK'S KETTLE
3141 16th Street, San Francisco,
CA 94103
monkskettle.com

◆

21ST AMENDMENT BREWERY
563 2nd Street, San Francisco,
CA 94107
21st-amendment.com

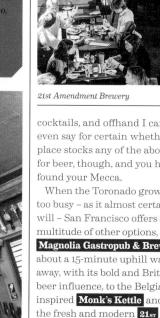

21st Amendment Brewery

cocktails, and offhand I can't even say for certain whether the place stocks any of the above. Go for beer, though, and you have found your Mecca.

When the Toronado grows too busy – as it almost certainly will – San Francisco offers a multitude of other options, from **Magnolia Gastropub & Brewery** about a 15-minute uphill walk away, with its bold and British beer influence, to the Belgian-inspired **Monk's Kettle** and the fresh and modern **21st Amendment Brewery** near the ballpark. And if those are also full, simply walk down the road a bit, because one of the great things about San Francisco is that there is almost always something new and interesting waiting around the next corner.

TAKING LIBERTIES
IN SAN DIEGO

San Diego's **Stone Brewing** is known for big beers and even bigger ideas. Founded in 1996 with a strong, hop-forward – and highly unlikely – flagship ale called Arrogant Bastard, Stone outgrew its original facility within its first decade and moved on to much larger premises in nearby Escondido, opening its brewery-side World Bistro & Gardens a year later. Other expansions followed, as did other San Diego-area outlets and, eventually, other production breweries, one on the other side of the country in Richmond, Virginia, and another in Berlin, Germany.

While all of these moves were ambitious to varying degrees, arguably the one with the biggest imprint on the beer travel map was the May 2013 opening of the **World Bistro & Gardens – Liberty Station**. Built in the former Naval Training Center near San Diego International Airport, Stone Liberty Station is sufficiently large that it makes the expansive World Bistro at the Escondido brewery appear almost diminutive, with new rooms, halls and outdoor spaces seemingly appearing around every corner. San Diego having the dry and temperate climate that it does, that means just over 2,000m² (½ acre) of year-round eating and drinking space.

Of course, the wood-beamed, high-ceilinged rooms, bocce ball courts and outdoor theatre space are mere distractions from the main draw at Liberty Station: the beer. In total, there are 75 taps pouring throughout the complex; 40 are available at the indoor bar, 31 at the outdoor garden bar and an additional four at the theatre. And while, sure, most are pouring beers brewed either at Liberty Station or Escondido, there are also regular appearances of ales and lagers from other, mostly southern California, breweries such as Modern Times and

Stone Brewing World Bistro & Gardens – Liberty Station

Liberty Public Market

dozens of shops and restaurants, and you have the makings of a fairly outstanding southern California day.

WHILE YOU'RE THERE

San Diego is chock-a-block with brewery taps and beer bars, but for a relaxed afternoon there is none much better than **Half Door Brewing Company**, a downtown brewpub that somehow stays just under the radar in the oft-overhyped local beer scene.

Port Brewing, and even the occasional out-of-state brew from the likes of Colorado's Avery or Michigan's Jolly Pumpkin.

Pair several hours spent at the brewery-restaurant with a visit to the recently opened **Liberty Public Market**, itself the size of Liberty Station and featuring

ADDRESS BOOK

STONE BREWING WORLD BISTRO & GARDENS – LIBERTY STATION
2816 Historic Decatur Road, San Diego, CA 92106
stonebrewing.com

◆

LIBERTY PUBLIC MARKET
2820 Historic Decatur Road, San Diego, CA 92106
libertypublicmarket.com

◆

HALF DOOR BREWING COMPANY
903 Island Avenue, San Diego, CA 92101
halfdoorbrewing.com

Half Door Brewing

LAND OF DARKNESS
AND STRONG BEER

Unless you're the kind of person who really likes the cold – and I mean *really* likes it – it would probably take quite a bit of convincing to talk you into flying to Anchorage, Alaska, in the dead of winter. But before you rule it out completely, consider the following phrase: the **Great Alaska Beer & Barley Wine Festival**.

It takes a lot to get through an Alaskan winter, when the temperatures drop and the sun rises only enough to peek over the horizon for a couple of hours. A lot of fortitude and perseverance, for certain; a lot of warm clothing, definitely; and for those so inclined, a lot of very strong beer. Which is what the Beer & Barley Wine Fest, now almost a quarter-century old, is all about.

In a way, it is precisely this forbidding environment that makes the festival in Anchorage such a draw, since the combination of dark and cold adds a certain majesty to the event, making it feel more like a rite of passage than just another beer festival. Add strong and not-so-strong beers from across Alaska, the other states

ADDRESS BOOK

GREAT ALASKA BEER & BARLEY WINE FESTIVAL
William A. Egan Civic & Convention Center, Anchorage, AK 99501
auroraproductions.net/beer-barley.html
◆
HUMPY'S GREAT ALASKAN ALEHOUSE
610 West 6th Avenue, Anchorage, AK 99501
humpysalaska.com

and even well beyond and you have the makings of three most entertaining and enjoyable tasting sessions scattered over two days.

Of course, the biggest attraction is the barley wines, which have become a bit of an Alaskan speciality. (In fact, partly because of the festival, Arctic Devil Barley Wine by Anchorage's Midnight Sun Brewing has grown into something of a legend.) Most breweries bring theirs, and some make special-release barley wines just for the fest. For those less enamoured with potent ales,

there is also a multitude of lower-strength beers and even a handful of ciders from which to choose, but most attendees head for the stronger stuff – particularly toward the completion of each tasting session.

There is no strategy to a festival such as this, except to pace oneself, give a wide berth to those not pacing themselves, and generally go with festive flow. For tomorrow will once again be dark and cold, so you might as well celebrate today.

WHILE YOU'RE THERE
It would be a shame to travel all the way to Anchorage and not pay a visit to **Humpy's Great Alaskan Alehouse**, a beer bar and pub with not only the state's largest selection of beer on tap, but enough style and allure to be a beer destination of note in almost any state.

Winter weather can be nasty in Anchorage, but it never snows at the Alehouse or beer fest!

A GREAT MEAL IN DALLAS

For years, one of the biggest secrets in American beer circles was Dallas, Texas. The US South and Southwest in general and Texas in particular were slow to take to craft beer, and so developments in the Lone Star State – outside of ever-funky Austin, at least – for the most part happened without eliciting much in the way of aficionado fanfare.

Among the first major moves was the opening of what is now the state's oldest craft brewery, Houston's Saint Arnold Brewing, in 1994, followed by the founding and slow expansion of the Flying Saucer Draught Emporium chain of pioneering southern beer bars. A handful of other breweries then opened over the course of the balance of the 1990s before progress more or less ground to, if not a complete halt, at least a very slow roll. That lasted for a decade or so.

As the century progressed into its second decade, however, Dallas quietly came into its own as a southwest hub of great craft beer, with the opening of breweries such as Peticolas Brewing, Community Beer Co., the now-Molson Coors-owned Revolver Brewing, and chronically underestimated Martin House Brewing. And in support of it all, a shifting family of Flying Saucers and one terrific offshoot, The Meddlesome Moth in downtown Dallas.

Founded by the owners of the Saucer group, the Moth was as pioneering for Dallas when it opened in 2010 as the first Saucers were in the 1990s. In addition to being the first restaurant of note to open in the only-just-emerging Design District, the partners had the temerity to combine 40 draught taps and a lengthy bottled-beer list with white linen and stained-glass art, topping it off

Above & right: The Meddlesome Moth

with a menu long on creativity and short on "pub grub".

That said, a meal at the Moth is precisely what you wish to make of it – a lengthy repast of fine cuisine partnered with specific complementary beers, or a pint and a burger, albeit one made from grass-fed beef. What separates it from the average gastropub is Moth partner and beer guru Keith Schlabs's meticulously chosen beer list, which highlights

Community Beer Company

many of the local beer scene's rapidly rising stars, but not at the expense of a rounded and encompassing selection.

Put it all together, add in a most amenable restaurant-side patio, and you have an equation that adds up to a very solid Lone Star State beer destination, with the added advantage of the **Community Beer Company** being located just down the road.

ADDRESS BOOK

THE MEDDLESOME MOTH
1621 Oak Lawn Avenue, Dallas, TX 75207
mothinthe.net

◆

COMMUNITY BEER COMPANY
1530 Inspiration Drive, Dallas, TX 75207
communitybeer.com

CRAFT BEER
24/7 IN NEW ORLEANS

Back in the 1990s, it was possible to identify most, if not all, dedicated beer bars in the United States. At the very least, it was a simple endeavour to tick off all the important places to visit for beer in any particular city. Most such places at the time bore a great resemblance to one another. They were usually fairly ramshackle joints, the result of having been pieced together on a shoestring by budget-conscious beer-enthusiast entrepreneurs, and they were open from sometime in the afternoon until the local legal closing hour, lunches deemed to have been of negligible profitability for a place specializing in beer.

Today, of course, beer bars are in abundance in not just every major North American city, but almost every district of every city. Still, there are those that remain apart from the crowd. One such establishment is the immensely laudable Avenue Pub in the Garden District of New Orleans, to my knowledge the only beer bar in

The Avenue Pub

Music is as much a part of New Orleans life as food and, of course, beer.

ADDRESS BOOK

THE AVENUE PUB
1732 St Charles Avenue,
New Orleans, LA 70130
theavenuepub.com

◆

ABITA BREWERY VISITOR
CENTER & TAP ROOM
166 Barbee Road, Covington,
LA 70433
abita.com

the world that is open 24 hours a day, seven days a week.

But it's not just the temporal uniqueness of the Avenue that makes it special, and neither is it the selection of beers the pub offers, which in my experience is the best in the Big Easy by a long shot. No, what really elevates the Avenue to the status of truly special is the example set by its owner, Polly Watts, whose inspiringly upbeat attitude apparently infects all of the pub's staff and makes it not just a great beer bar, but a great bar – period.

As anyone who has visited New Orleans will know, the city hardly needs beer to recommend it as a travel destination, as full as it is with culture and cuisine and simple fun. But if you do find yourself heading "down the Mississippi down to New Orleans", plan for an evening, or afternoon, or overnight, at The Avenue Pub. It will add a dimension to your trip you couldn't even have imagined would exist.

WHILE YOU'RE THERE

Most people visiting New Orleans will be loath to leave the city, but a case can certainly be made for renting a car for a day trip or, preferably, overnight visit, to nearby Covington, home of the **Abita Brewery**. Although not usually listed on the beer-geek hierarchy of breweries, Abita does many things very well and puts on a terrific tour to boot.

AN EXCELLENT REASON
NOT TO STAY
IN ATLANTA

Many people who visit Atlanta will stay within the downtown district, or perhaps venture as far north as the Buckhead neighbourhood, home to many of the city's most revered restaurants. But a lucky few will know to board the Metropolitan Atlanta Rapid Transit Authority, or MARTA, train and take it east to Decatur, where they will find the Georgian equivalent of beer nirvana.

Exiting the station, you will find yourself within a two-minute walk of Decatur Square and the appropriately red-brick-clad **Brick Store Pub**. Pass through its front door and you will understand why you have come to Decatur. A horseshoe-shaped bar dominates the main floor of the pub affectionately known as "the Brick", where you will be able to order one of 29 draught beers, which, on the surface, frankly, doesn't sound like that many. But the 20-year-old Brick has not gotten to where it is today by stocking just any old selection of ales and lagers, so when the bar's website states that its taps present only a "carefully chosen" array of beers, you can be assured it is no idle boast.

ADDRESS BOOK

BRICK STORE PUB
125 E. Court Square, Decatur,
GA 30030
brickstorepub.com
◆
LEON'S FULL SERVICE
131 E Ponce de Leon Avenue,
Decatur, GA 30030
leonsfullservice.com

The downstairs focus is on a mix of American craft and select imported draught beers, although you may discover at any time a selection of obscure collaboration brews, a treasured rarity, or even limited editions produced exclusively for the pub. But perhaps you're feeling a bit Belgian – in which case you can venture upstairs to the Belgian bar, established in 2004 when the Georgia legislature finally relented and allowed for the legal sale of beer above 6% ABV in the state.

Turning left after your climb, you'll be greeted by a mere eight draught selections, but Belgian beer generally being more bottle-focused than it is keg-friendly, those taps will be supplemented by a list of more than 120 bottled brands. And if some studiously aged beer strikes your fancy, to the right of the stairs sits the Beer Cellar, home to hundreds of vintage brews dating back as old as the pub itself.

Food at the Brick is of good quality, but the kitchen is decidedly casual and pub-oriented in its approach. If you desire something a bit more sophisticated, around the corner awaits **Leon's Full Service**, with its southern take on Belgian-French brasserie fare. And since there is shared ownership between the two places, you can rest easy in the knowledge that while Leon's beer selection is but a fraction of the Brick's, it is every bit as carefully assembled.

Leon's Full Service

A BIT OF INDIA
IN NASHVILLE

If a modern and innovative Indian restaurant might seem like a bit of an anomaly for the city known the world over for the Grand Ole Opry and the Country Music Hall of Fame, then such a restaurant with an associated brewery charged with making Indian food-friendly beers would likely appear doubly so. But such a place does reside among the music bars and songwriter workshops of Nashville, thanks to the apparently tireless chef Maneet Chauhan and her eponymous restaurant and **Mantra Artisan Ales**.

Knowing innately that Indian food partners well with beer, the award-winning cookbook author, television personality and chef partnered herself with two young and aspiring brewers to create a brewery where harmonies with Indian cuisine were, if not exactly guiding principles, at least a significant concern. Out of that partnership Mantra was born.

The brewery and its taproom may be found in Franklin, about a half-hour drive outside of Nashville, but most of its beers are also available at the **Chauhan Ale & Masala House**, sandwiched between downtown

Chauhan Ale & Masala House

ADDRESS BOOK

MANTRA ARTISAN ALES
216 Noah Drive #140, Franklin, TN 37064
mantrabrewing.com
◆

CHAUHAN ALE & MASALA HOUSE
123 12th Avenue North, Nashville, TN 37203
chauhannashville.com
◆

SMITH & LENTZ BREWING
903 Main Street, Nashville, TN 37206
smithandlentz.com

and Music Row. There, you can partake not only of such memorable and unusual beers as the self-describing Saffron IPA and the unique Japa Milk Chai Stout, brewed with a custom blend of chai spices, but also one of the most interesting, fun and delicious menus I have come across at an Indian restaurant. Think Tandoori Chicken Poutine and Malabari Seafood Cioppino, made with coconut garam masala broth, and you begin to get an idea of what the food is all about.

Best of all, given that the beer was designed with the food in mind, you get to combine the two in ways that are sometimes surprising and almost always wonderfully harmonious, creating an experience that is worth the trip to Music City on its own.

WHILE YOU'RE THERE
For a more conventional but no less attractive beer experience, head over to East Nashville to the spare but welcoming confines of **Smith & Lentz Brewing**, where the El Cuarto IPA will dazzle with aromas of pineapple and papaya, and the occasionally featured pilsner or Vienna lager is not to be missed.

AND A TOUCH OF GERMANY
IN CINCINNATI

There are two things you need to know about the German style of lager known as *bock*. Done well, *bocks* are singularly delicious examples of the brewing arts. Also, they are not produced by brewers outside of Germany with anywhere near the frequency they deserve.

Which brings us to the spring **Bockfest** in Cincinnati, Ohio. For one glorious weekend in March, a time when warming, strong-ish beer like *bock* is certainly deserving of attention in the US Midwest, Cincinnati beer drinkers give themselves over to the worship of *bock*. The hub is the transformed Christian Moerlein Brewery in the district known as Over-the-Rhine, changed for the weekend into Bockfest Hall, but that is just the tip of the city's impressive *bockbier* iceberg of events. Across town, parades are held, Sausage Queen and Beard Baron are crowned, dinners are hosted and tours guided, polkas are danced and, of course, beers are enjoyed. Lots of beers. *Bock* beers.

After which, according to local brewers, most people go back to drinking lagers and pale ales and IPAs and ignore the very *bocks* they just finished venerating. Which, I suppose, explains why more aren't brewed around Ohio, the Midwest and throughout the United States.

WHILE YOU ARE THERE
It isn't one of Bockfest's official venues, possibly because it's actually located across the Ohio River in Newport, Kentucky, but, to further your Germanic experience, a trip to the nearby **Hofbräuhaus Newport** is definitely recommended. It was the first offshoot of the famed Munich beer hall in the United States and remains a very fine beer destination.

ADDRESS BOOK

BOCKFEST, CINCINNATI
bockfest.com
◆
HOFBRÄUHAUS NEWPORT
*3rd & Saratoga at the Levee,
200 East 3rd Street, Newport,
KY 41071
hofbrauhausnewport.com*

Above: Parading during Bockfest. Opposite: Downtown Cincinnati.

ASHEVILLE:
THE UNEXPECTED BEER CITY

When, in early 2012, California's Sierra Nevada Brewing announced plans to build a new facility in Asheville, North Carolina, a lot of people connected to the US brewing industry responded, "Where?" The small city at the foot of the Great Smoky Mountains was not exactly shining bright on the craft-beer radar.

Boy, has that changed! In the wake of Sierra Nevada's announcement, both New Belgium Brewing and Oskar Blues announced their intentions to build breweries in the area, and for a time it looked like that trio might be joined by Oregon powerhouse Deschutes. (Deschutes eventually chose to build in Roanoke, Virginia.) This is in addition to roughly 30 local area breweries, including some, like the now Anheuser-Busch InBev-owned Wicked Weed and Green Man, that number among the most admired in the eastern United States.

Water quality and abundance have something to do with Asheville's popularity among brewers, as does access to major north-south and east-west transportation routes. But a lot, too, has to do with quality of life, the community of brewers and a general passion for beer among the local citizenry. All of which have made Asheville a beer city that is as praiseworthy as it is unexpected.

Approaches to Asheville vary – should you focus on beer bars like the Thirsty Monk and Bier Garden? Or check out the wonderful shop Bruisin' Ales? Maybe stick to breweries? But there is little question that the most time-efficient approach is to focus upon the South Slope

Above: You never need walk far for a great beer in Asheville. Right: Thirsty Monk.

neighbourhood. There, within about a fifteen-minute walk, you will find over a dozen breweries nestled in an area that was formerly home to nothing but warehouses and industrial developments.

The Wicked Weed taproom and separate Funkatorium might be Big Beer possessions now, but that does nothing to detract from what locals are beginning to call the Brewery District. Not when Burial Brewing's original location is smack in the middle of the Slope's taproom crawl and the estimable Hi-Wire Brewing is also present, not to mention the slightly variable Catawba Brewing and Twin Leaf, and veteran operations Green Man and Asheville Brewing. There may exist cities where a greater number of breweries reside within closer approximation, but they are few, if any.

Indeed, the wonderful thing about not just the South Slope

Above: Wicked Weed. Top: Funkatorium

but all of Asheville is that you're pretty much guaranteed to run out of drinking capacity before you exhaust the list of stellar places in which to drink.

WHERE TO STAY

For comfort and proximity to the South Slope, it's difficult to beat the **Aloft Asheville Downtown**, ideally positioned between the breweries and downtown.

ADDRESS BOOK

For more on Asheville's many brewers, visit the Asheville Brewers Alliance at avlbrewers.com

ALOFT ASHEVILLE DOWNTOWN
51 Biltmore Avenue, Asheville, NC 28801
aloftashevilledowntown.com

BREWING IN
THE SHADOW
OF A GIANT

T he largest beer company in the world is Anheuser-Busch InBev. It is a monstrously massive company, by some estimates responsible for more than one out of every four beers consumed on this planet. And its spiritual home in the United States is St. Louis, Missouri.

Even before Anheuser-Busch was consumed by Belgian-Brazilian company InBev, and before that two-headed giant went on to devour global number-two brewer SABMiller, brewing in the presence of the domineering powerhouse that is Budweiser must have been daunting. And indeed it was most likely the reason that the St. Louis Brewery, better known as Schlafly Beer, was for years after its 1991 opening the only other brewing company in town.

While the company has grown out of its original premises, that brewpub still exists as the **Schlafly Tap Room**, a most pleasant pub in a restored, 100-year-old brick-and-timber building. In recent years, however, its influence on the urban beer scene has been overshadowed by the presence of others.

Above: 4 Hands Brewing. Top: Schlafly Tap Room

ADDRESS BOOK

SCHLAFLY TAP ROOM
2100 Locust Street, St. Louis,
MO 63103
schlafly.com
◆

PERENNIAL ARTISAN ALES
8125 Michigan Avenue,
St. Louis, MO 63111
perennialbeer.com
◆

URBAN CHESTNUT MIDTOWN
BREWERY & BIERGARTEN
3229 Washington Avenue,
St. Louis, MO 63103
(& two other locations)
urbanchestnut.com
◆

4 HANDS BREWING COMPANY
1220 South 8th Street, St. Louis,
MO 63104
4handsbrewery.com

Schlafly Tap Toom

Two not-to-be-missed breweries are **Perennial** and **Urban Chestnut**, the latter with a trio of outlets, each slightly more Germanic than the last. Which makes sense, because Urban Chestnut brewmaster and visionary Florian Kuplent began his brewing career in Germany and pays homage to that heritage through his clever cross-pollination of German beer styles and American influence. Zwickel, Kuplent's unfiltered lager, is a wonderful ode to Bavaria, while beers like Winged Nut, a chestnut ale fermented with *weissbier* yeast, mixes things up a bit.

Perennial's tasting room is certainly a bit more rustic than the urban-beerhall ambience you'll discover at any of the Urban Chestnuts, but then again, so are its beers. Located in south St. Louis, it offers nibbles like pâté platters, pretzels and grilled cheese to go with ales like the nutty, subtly funky Aria and chamomile-spiced Saison du Lis. If you're downtown without a car, it can be a tricky place to reach, but worth the effort.

Much more central is **4 Hands Brewing**, another St. Louis brewing force that appeared only within the past half-decade or so. Located a mere 15-minute walk from Busch Stadium – there's the influence of that giant again – it offers ample seating in its recently expanded, industrial-cool tasting room, as well as beers to quench your post-game thirst, like the superbly balanced pale ale City Wide, and others to broaden your experience, such as the War Hammer Imperial IPA with its layers of marmalade and fruit flavours.

With breweries like these operating in its shadow, it's little wonder that sales of AB InBev's flagship Budweiser and Bud Light have been in decline in recent years.

CHICAGO BEER BY THE "L"

The taproom at Half Acre Beer Company.

It's hard to say precisely when the breweries began piling up in Chicago, but by the time this century's second decade had commenced, it was obvious that the City of the Big Shoulders was well on its way to becoming the City of the Big Beers.

That's the good news. The bad news is that visitors determined to stick to the prime downtown areas of the Loop and the Magnificent Mile are destined to miss the best of what the city has to offer. Because to really earn your craft-beer stripes in Chi-Town, you need to climb aboard the "L", as the above-ground train system is commonly known.

On the Brown line, the first stop is Irving Park, gateway to a trio of particularly impressive breweries. A roughly five-minute stroll from the station will bring you to **Begyle Brewing**, a local fave serving ten or so beers that range from good to very good, including the recommended mainstay, the citrus and tropical fruity Crash Landed Pale Wheat Ale, in a relaxed and airy taproom. One block further is the immediately impressive **Dovetail Brewery**, born in the spring of 2016. Specializing in German-style lagers and wheat beers, its taproom is darker but somehow more harmonious than that of Begyle and its beers will transport you to Bavaria even if you've never

ADDRESS BOOK

BEGYLE BREWING
1800 West Cuyler Avenue,
Chicago, IL 60613
begylebrewing.com

◆

DOVETAIL BREWERY
1800 West Belle Plaine,
Chicago, IL 60613
dovetailbrewery.com

◆

HALF ACRE BEER COMPANY
4257 North Lincoln Avenue,
Chicago, IL 60618
halfacrebeer.com

◆

REVOLUTION BREWING
2323 North Milwaukee Avenue,
Chicago, IL 60647
revbrew.com

◆

PIECE BREWERY & PIZZERIA
1927 West North Avenue,
Chicago, IL 60622
piecechicago.com

◆

HAYMARKET PUB & BREWERY
737 West Randolph Street,
Chicago, IL 60661
haymarketbrewing.com

Haymarket

Outside Half Acre.

set foot in Germany. In particular, the Munich-style pale lager, simply called Lager, is sublime in its elegant straightforwardness.

Ten minutes of further walking will take you to the **Half Acre Beer Company**, one of Chicago's most revered breweries. Begin with a glass of the flagship pale ale, Daisy Cutter, fruity and eminently quaffable, then work your way through samplers of a few of the 14 available taps, ending at the Navaja Double IPA, terrifically balanced for a beer of 9.5% ABV.

Over on the Blue line, meanwhile, **Revolution Brewing** is at California station. A fully

licensed brewpub with an extensive dining menu, it's a popular after-work destination, with a superb, spicy and best bitter-ish Fist City and stronger Anti-Hero IPA among many other offerings.

Two stops south at Damen, you will find **Piece**, a brewery and pizzeria that excels equally at both disciplines, where you can treat yourself to pie and a glass of The Weight, a zestily bitter pale ale. Or take that same train all the way to Grand and walk six blocks south to the **Haymarket Pub & Brewery** for a burger and a pint of The Defender American

Stout, creamy with roasted chocolate notes.

Consider that the above covers just two of Chicago's eight L-lines, representing a fraction of the city's many breweries, and you begin to appreciate just how much the city now has to offer. Better make it a long weekend – or maybe even a week if you want to get a handle on the whole scene.

THE BREWERY ON THE HILL

outhwest of the college town of Madison, in the state of Wisconsin, stands a small village of Swiss extraction, home to just over 2,000 people. Were it not for one particular defining attraction, it is the sort of town one might drive through, thinking, "This seems lovely and quaint, but not quite worth a stop."

And if you did not care about beer, that's precisely what you'd be likely to do. If, on the other hand, you are the sort of person who will travel for beer, you are likely to be in New Glarus for one very specific reason: the **New Glarus Brewing Company**.

Founded in 1993 by brewer Daniel Carey and his wife, Deborah, known to all as Dan and Deb, New Glarus the brewery has followed a curious and, in some ways, highly unusual path for growth. Beginning in a small brewery on the edge of town, the duo set their focus on a single flagship beer, the now-Wisconsin-wide Spotted Cow golden ale, while rounding out their portfolio with a wide range of supporting stars, such as the Wisconsin Belgian Red cherry ale and seasonal specialities like Uff-da Bock.

ADDRESS BOOK

NEW GLARUS BREWING COMPANY
2400 State Highway 69,
New Glarus, WI 53574
newglarusbrewing.com
◆
PUEMPEL'S OLDE TAVERN
18 6th Avenue, New Glarus,
WI 53574
puempels.com

Nothing particularly odd about that strategy, of course. As success befell the brewery, however, the Careys decided that, rather than chase markets with their much-coveted fruit-beer range, they would confine their sales to Wisconsin alone, not even venturing as far as Rockford, Illinois, a mere 60 miles (97km) south.

The strategy worked like a charm. The company quickly outgrew the original brewery and moved to a purpose-built – and quite lovely – brewery atop a nearby hill, with free self-guided brewery tours, a large beer garden and expansive grounds open to the public

for picnicking and outdoor recreation. Deb's stated ambition was to make a centre for her community, open to one and all, and that is exactly what she has accomplished.

Then there are the beers. Few breweries in the United States or beyond can boast a similar level of excellence across a wide range of styles, from what many, myself included, consider to be the best spontaneously fermented beers in the US – brewed in the original facility, now known as the Wild Fruit Cave – to *bocks*, wheat beers of several styles, stout and brown ale, IPA and double-IPA and, of course, fruit beers.

Were it just for the beers alone, New Glarus would be more than worth a visit. Add in the charms of the brewery and its surrounding village and you have as close to a can't-miss beer destination as exists in North America.

WHILE YOU ARE THERE

After your brewery visit, don't forget to stroll into town for a beer or two at **Puempel's Olde Tavern**, a mural-clad, late 19th-century tavern that has changed little over the last one hundred years.

SLEEPING AT THE BREWERY

There are a lot of things you can do at a modern brewery. Many have taprooms where you can drink. Some also offer food, from nibbles to complete meals. A bunch provide games, from darts and the beanbag-toss game known as Cornhole to vintage pinball and video games, and some even have children's play areas. What most do not offer is a place to sleep. Which is where Milwaukee's **Brewhouse Inn & Suites** comes in.

Housed in the multi-building complex that was once home to the Pabst Brewing Company, the Brewhouse Inn is not just built into some random gutted and retro-fitted building, but actually occupies the old Pabst brewhouse. And if this fact is not apparent as you approach the hotel, turning corners around identifiably old, yellow brick buildings and checking in at a desk clad in old glass bottle bottoms, it certainly becomes clear when you lean over the upstairs railing to find massive copper brew kettles lining the atrium below.

Those kettles are actually from the old brewery, beautifully

The unusual lobby at the Brewhouse Inn & Suites. Overleaf: Milwaukee

restored and occupying an inordinate amount of space one imagines could easily have been given over to another

purpose. Combined with the soaring ceilings, reclaimed and repurposed wood and metal pieces and a signature stained-glass depiction of one of brewing's many real and imagined patron saints, King Gambrinus, they deliver an unmistakable sense of the local and national importance the building once boasted.

But no one sleeps in an atrium (at least not intentionally), so the theme continues in the luxurious rooms and suites, with "bubbly" French doors decorated to resemble beer, industrial and Victorian-chic stylings and plenty of exposed brick and wood. Combined, it delivers a tangible air of history with all the comfort and convenience of a modern, high-end hotel.

WHILE YOU'RE THERE

Without question, one of the best brewery tours in the United States is the one at **Lakefront Brewery**, which not only emphasizes fun and entertainment, but even schedules an intermission so that glasses might be refilled at the bar.

ADDRESS BOOK

BREWHOUSE INN & SUITES
1215 North 10th Street,
Milwaukee, WI 53205
brewhousesuites.com
◆

LAKEFRONT BREWERY
1872 North Commerce Street,
Milwaukee, WI 53212
lakefrontbrewery.com

TWO BREWERIES
IN KALAMAZOO

Admittedly, Kalamazoo, Michigan, is not a place many people might think to visit for fun. Located at the base of the "Michigan mitt", it's more than a two-hour drive from Chicago or Detroit – longer when traffic is heavy. And while it does share an airport with Battle Creek, most flights originate from the two big cities anyway. Once reached, however, the city of 75,000 ably shows its not-inconsiderable charm, at least when the weather is cooperative, with an easily walkable and attractive downtown, ample

Pouring at the Eccentric Café.

surrounding green space and, of course, a fair amount of beer.

There are 14 breweries within the greater Kalamazoo area, six of which are located within walking distance of one another downtown. While I would never

be one to discourage brewery explorations, a person could be quite content visiting just two of them. The mandatory visit in Kalamazoo will come as no surprise to anyone who has paid attention to American craft beer over the past several decades. It is to the **Eccentric Café**, run by the 30-plus-year-old Midwestern icon, Bell's Brewery.

Opened on 11 June 1993, not quite eight years after brewery founder Larry Bell sold his first commercial beer, the Eccentric Café sits beside the company's original and still active brewery in what, Bell recalls, was once a fairly rough area. Today, following a decades-long downtown revitalization project, the café is a neighbourhood lynchpin, with a restaurant, beer garden, pub and The Back Room, the facility's live music venue.

Over 40 taps deliver a multitude of Bell's beer, from long-standing favourites like the intense and darkly fruity Expedition Stout to brewpub exclusives, which the kitchen complements with a menu ranging from charcuterie to burgers made from locally sourced, grass-fed beef and a variety of finger foods. As engaging as the Eccentric Café

Arcadia Ales

The beer hall at the Eccentric Café.

ADDRESS BOOK

ECCENTRIC CAFÉ & GENERAL STORE
355 East Kalamazoo Avenue, Kalamazoo, MI 49007
bellsbeer.com

◆

ARCADIA ALES
701 East Michigan Avenue, Kalamazoo, MI 49007
arcadiaales.com

might be, however, its far newer, down-the-road neighbour might be even more so.

Established in 1996 in nearby Battle Creek, **Arcadia Ales** opened its main production brewery in early 2014, just an eight-minute walk from the Eccentric Café. Its pub, located at one end of the brewery, appears oddly nondescript from the road, but once entered opens up to an expansive, airy indoor space with a gorgeous beer garden along the banks of the Kalamazoo River. Food at Arcadia comes from the on site smoker and matches up with the brewery's beer in wonderful ways, from the beef brisket and interestingly floral Imperial Stout to the pulled pork and spicy Sky High Rye.

Together, these two fine operations might just be Kalamazoo's greatest tourism draw, and are each most certainly worth the drive from Chicago.

THE GENTLE CHARMS OF
BURLINGTON, VERMONT

Vermont made its mark upon the US craft-beer scene in two parts. Stage one highlighted a handful of early, but for the time prolific, breweries, including the now-defunct Catamount, Magic Hat (which has since become part of North American Breweries) and the late Greg Noonan's Vermont Pub & Brewery. While they weren't massive in number, they were perhaps disproportionally influential in the development of East Coast craft beer.

Stage two happened more recently and, depending on your perspective, perhaps ignominiously. The New England IPA, as it is now widely termed, got its cloudy, olfactory start as Vermont IPA, and its impact on the world of North

The Farmhouse

American IPAs is not to be discounted in the short term, although the jury is still very much out with respect to the long term.

In the middle of both stages, however, has been, and still is, Burlington, the state's largest city and one of the US Northeast's most unfailingly attractive and pleasant. With a population of only around 42,000 as of 2015, Burlington is a charming and wonderfully walkable city, or at least it is when not in the depths of winter. Being small, it is not as replete with beer bars and

breweries as are cities five, ten or 20 times its size, but like the bar with a dozen well-chosen taps can prove superior to the one with 100, sometimes less really can be more.

The cream of the local beer bar crop is **The Farmhouse**, a restaurant and bar that is as restful in summer on its backyard beer garden as it is cosy in its low-lit parlour during the wintertime. Of course, an extensive draught, cask and bottled beer list doesn't hurt, especially when it is complemented by a fine array of ciders, wines by the glass and refreshingly affordable cocktails.

ADDRESS BOOK

THE FARMHOUSE TAP & GRILL
160 Bank Street, Burlington,
VT 05401
farmhousetg.com

◆

ZERO GRAVITY BREWPUB AT
AMERICAN FLATBREAD
115 Saint Paul Street, Burlington,
VT 05401
zerogravitybeer.com

◆

VERMONT PUB & BREWERY
144 College Street, Burlington,
VT 05401
vermontbrewery.com

◆

HOTEL VERMONT
41 Cherry Street, Burlington,
VT 05401
hotelvt.com

If that doesn't suit, the unlikely union of the **Zero Gravity Craft Brewery** and the **American Flatbread** restaurant awaits only a few blocks away. And while it might not quite possess the allure it did back when it was the only game in town, the **Vermont Pub & Brewery** remains a strongly recommended visit.

Perhaps Burlington's best-kept secret, however, is that even non-beer-focused places tend to stock the local stuff, often including those much-sought-after rarities that people line up for elsewhere in the state. Strolling around town is not just a thoroughly pleasant experience, but also, potentially, a walk full of happy beer surprises.

WHERE TO STAY

Hotel Vermont is not only unquestionably the coolest and most comfortable lodging place in town, it is also home to Juniper, a lobby bar with a more than respectable selection of locally made beers and spirits.

Sampling beer at the Hotel Vermont.

THE BEST OF
BOSTONIAN BEER

At its core, Boston is a beer town, always has been and probably always will be. But where some modern beer cities are defined by their breweries, Boston has long been far more about its bars.

Oh sure, there are and have been breweries, such as the outstanding **Cambridge Brewing**, newcomer **Night Shift** in nearby Everett and the now-iconic **Boston Beer Company**, maker of the Sam Adams line of beers. But far beyond those, there has always been the city's bar scene, filled with a solid, if changeable, core of fine beer bars and a far larger grouping of splendid taverns, sports bars, Irish-style pubs and other assorted watering holes that just happened to serve great beer.

Of the fine beer bars, present standouts include **The Publick House**, a Belgian-leaning institution in Brookline; **Lord Hobo**, a stellar stop for beer, wine and cocktails in Cambridge; and the Back Bay's **Bukowski Tavern**, a somewhat worn but lovable beer den. It is the class of taverns that might just be the more interesting, though, beginning with places like **Row 34**, located near the Convention Center.

Built in a warehouse with high ceilings and ample natural light, Row 34's core philosophy is laid out quite concisely on its website: "If we could eat oysters and drink beer for every meal period, we probably would." Hard to argue with that, particularly when the selections range to nine or more different oyster varieties and two-dozen smartly chosen taps.

Only slightly further afield in South Boston is another recent arrival, **Worden Hall**. With 40 taps spanning an impressive array of styles and origins, Worden is part of the ongoing renaissance of "Southie", as the district is universally known. While beer is obviously given

Outside the Bukowski Tavern.

ADDRESS BOOK

CAMBRIDGE BREWING
1 Kendall Square, Building 100,
Cambridge, MA 02139
cambridgebrewingcompany.com
◆

NIGHT SHIFT BREWING
87 Santilli Highway, Everett,
MA 02149
nightshiftbrewing.com
◆

THE BOSTON BEER COMPANY
30 Germania Street,
Boston, MA 02130
samueladams.com/brewery-and-
craft/boston-brewery
◆

THE PUBLICK HOUSE
1648 Beacon Street, Washington
Square, Brookline, MA 02445
thepublickhousebeerbar.com
◆

LORD HOBO BEER BAR
92 Hampshire Street, Cambridge,
MA 02139
lordhobo.com

Night Shift Brewing

ADDRESS BOOK

BUKOWSKI TAVERN
*50 Dalton Street, Boston,
MA 02115*
bukowskitavern.net

◆

ROW 34
*383 Congress Street, Boston,
MA 02210*
row34.com

◆

WORDEN HALL
*22 West Broadway, Boston,
MA 02127*
wordenhall.com

◆

LONE STAR TACO BAR
*635 Cambridge Street,
Cambridge, MA 02141*
lonestar-boston.com

◆

J.J. FOLEY'S CAFÉ
*117 East Berkeley Street, Boston,
MA 02118*
jjfoleyscafe.com

pride of place, the tavern's 100-plus whiskey selection and solid, gastropub-esque menu are nothing to sneer at, either.

On the other side of downtown, in Cambridge, not far from Lord Hobo, the **Lone Star Taco Bar** is far from your usual *taqueria*. With 14 taps pouring domestic and imported beers chosen specifically for their taco-friendliness – including delights such as seldom-seen German imports Schlenkerla Helles and Andechs Vollbier – this is about as unassuming and unpretentious a good beer joint as you can get.

Finally, if you want to drink good beer and still get a taste of historic Boston, head to the South End and **J.J. Foley's Café**, a 107-year-old family-owned institution. You won't find the latest "wild ale" offering you've been hearing about, but you will get to pick from a handful of solid local brews in a place that is about as archetypically Bostonian as they come.

A beer sampler at Night Shift Brewing.

A SPECIAL
FRIDAY THE THIRTEENTH

There is definitely no shortage of great beer destinations in Philadelphia. Begin in the heart of downtown with spots like the legendary **Monk's Café**, Tria Café or Taproom, or venerable Khyber Pass; head north to the Northern Liberties and Fishtown for the Standard Tap and Kraftwork; or wander to the Museum District for spots like Bar Hygge or the Belgian Café, all among many, many others.

So you might wonder why I'd suggest venturing well into the city's northeast to visit the **Grey Lodge Public House**. And my answer would be: because it's Friday the Thirteenth!

Or, more specifically, Friday the Firkinteenth. Which is the one – or two or three, depending on the number of Friday the Thirteenths on the calendar – day of the year that Grey Lodge owner Mike "Scoats" Scotese stocks his bar with all manner of cask-conditioned beers and pours them from morning until close. It's not the best cask-ale festival you will ever experience, but given the celebratory atmosphere and

community spirit of the event, it might just be the most fun.

Then again, there really isn't any reason to wait until a Firkinteenth to visit the Grey Lodge. Scoats has transformed

a basic working stiffs' bar of the sort I imagine the Philly version of Archie Bunker might have enjoyed in the 1970s into, well, a still-basic bar that just happens to stock some very good beers and be decorated by a seemingly ever-growing array of tongue-in-cheek mosaic murals.

It all combines to create the sort of place that begets lost afternoons that bleed into unproductive, but highly enjoyable, evenings. And if you need a reason beyond that to visit, then there is always the Firkinteenth, the pub's annual Groundhog Day celebrations or any of a number

Quiet times at the Grey Lodge.

ADDRESS BOOK

MONK'S CAFE
264 South 16th Street,
Philadelphia, PA 19102
monkscafe.com

◆

THE GREY LODGE PUB
6235 Frankford Avenue,
Philadelphia, PA 19135
greylodge.com

Above: The back room at Monk's Cafe sometimes hosts exclusive beer tastings.
Top: The Belgian awning of Monk's Cafe, a familiar sight to many beer travellers.

of fun and usually oddball occasions that Scoats deems necessary to celebrate.

WHILE YOU'RE THERE

As noted, Philadelphia is awash with beer destinations, but even so the aforementioned and pioneering Monk's Café is one particularly deserving of mention, with a solid and extensive beer list and an always impressive cuisine.

THE BEER ROOTS OF
THE BIG APPLE

You can say what you will about the notorious world-weariness of New Yorkers, but once they finally do embrace something, be it a culinary trend or new art form, they do so with gusto. And so it came to pass that what was one of the last major cities in the United States to realize that craft brewing was a going concern has now become home to a multitude of excellent destinations for beer, with dozens in Manhattan alone and plenty more in the surrounding boroughs.

As such, there are far more than may be responsibly listed here. Still, there remain some venerable places of note. After separate tragedies claimed the lives of both the original owners of the pioneering East Village beer bar **d.b.a.**, the place seemed to lose some of its edge, so that while it remains a more than respectable place to "drink good stuff", as per its long-standing motto, it is no longer the outstanding beer destination it once was. Fortunately, there is still the **Blind Tiger**.

Since its forced move from its original digs in 2005–06, the Tiger has only gotten better,

Gramercy Tavern

with now 28 draught taps filled with often difficult-to-find beers, mostly domestic craft ales, lagers and mixed-fermentation beers. More than the beer, though, the move gave the bar a superior ambience, with a stone fireplace as a focal point and wood salvaged from a 19th-century farm evoking the feel of a place much older than its actual age. Frequent events like the annual winter beer fest, Christmas in July, only add to its appeal.

For a more Manhattan feel, the **Gramercy Tavern** was one of the first "serious" restaurants in the United States to treat beer

Blind Tiger

ADDRESS BOOK

D.B.A.
41 First Avenue, New York, NY 10003
◆

BLIND TIGER
281 Bleecker Street, New York, NY 10014
blindtigeralehouse.com
◆

GRAMERCY TAVERN
42 East 20th Street, New York, NY 10003
gramercytavern.com
◆

RATTLE 'N' HUM (EAST)
14 East 33rd Street, New York, NY 10016
rattlenhumbarnyc.com/ rattlenhumeast
◆

RATTLE 'N' HUM (WEST)
306 West 39th Street, New York, NY 10018
rattlenhumbarnyc.com/ rattlenhumwest

Gramercy Tavern

with the respect it deserves, offering not only eight well-chosen taps, but also a vintage beer programme which, while pricey, provides carefully aged ales and lagers unobtainable elsewhere. In beer terms, a selection of cheeses enjoyed in the tavern alongside a vintage *doppelbock* or barley wine may be about as New York as it gets.

A decidedly different vibe is offered at the **Rattle 'N' Hum Bar**, which boasts similar locations on East 33rd and West 39th. Both offer homey atmospheres, 40 taps of craft beer and, refreshingly for these days, an approach to beer selection that is as international as it is loyal to the locals.

A THIRD
"GREAT" FESTIVAL

There are beer festivals in Canada that offer a greater number of beers for sampling, such as the Mondial de la Bière in Montréal. There are outdoor fests that are larger and more spread out, like the Toronto Festival of Beer. And there are festivals that are more tightly focused, like Cask Days in Toronto, or wide-ranging, like the Calgary International Beerfest. But to my knowledge and experience, there is no beer festival in the country that is more purely enjoyable than the **Great Canadian Beer Festival** (GCBF) in Victoria, British Columbia.

Held each year on the first weekend after Labour Day, slightly outside of downtown at the Royal Athletic Park, the GCBF might also be Canada's luckiest beer fest, given that, in the numerous years that have passed since the organizers moved the festival from December to September and inside to outside, it has experienced all of two instances of rain, neither lasting long nor interfering much with the enjoyment of the fest. With

Fancy dress at the Great Canadian Beer Festival.

The sun shines on the GCBF.

ADDRESS BOOK

GREAT CANADIAN BEER FESTIVAL
*Royal Athletic Park,
1014 Caledonia Avenue,
Victoria, BC V8T 1E8
gcbf.com*
◆

SPINNAKERS GASTRO BREWPUB & GUESTHOUSES
*308 Catherine Street, Victoria,
BC V9A 3S8
spinnakers.com*

tents scattered all around the park but with regularly far more attendees than tent space, this is no small factor in the festival's great and continued success.

A far greater factor, however, is the overall quality of the beer that festival planners Gerry Hieter, John Rowling and Phil Atkinson are able to secure for the event, which, while short of uniform excellence – what beer festival could possibly make such a claim? – is certainly superior to the average on display at most other Canadian beer events. It's a state of affairs helped by the fact that far more breweries regularly apply to pour than space permits.

Another feather in the GCBF's cap is the limit it places on ticket sales, which are kept to a very manageable number, despite the fact that a) the venue could definitely accommodate a larger crowd; and b) the festival regularly sells out on the same day tickets go on sale.

This results in an experience that, while hardly without queues, at least minimizes the claustrophobic crowding that besets all too many beer festivals around the world. Add in the fact that hotels in Victoria are remarkably reasonable around that time of year and you truly have a beer destination *par excellence*.

WHERE TO STAY
There are hotels in Victoria more luxurious and more convenient to downtown than **Spinnakers Gastro Brewpub & Guesthouses**, but no others offer the combination of idyllic situation on the north side of the harbour, a hearty "Brewer's Breakfast" to start your day and, of course, fresh beer brewed right next door.

Pouring at the festival.

CRAFT BEER REVOLUTION
IN VANCOUVER

Craft Brewing in Canada was born in Vancouver. The nation's first microbrewery was the city's now-Molson-Coors-owned Granville Island Brewing, and the modern brewpub in North America was born northwest of Vancouver at Horseshoe Bay. For a time in the 1990s, brewing thrived in and around the lower mainland. Until, that is, it didn't.

From the opening of the since-closed Dix brewpub in 1998, not a single brewery or brewpub opened in Vancouver for over a decade, according to Joe Wiebe's excellent British Columbia beer guide, *Craft Beer Revolution*. Sure, there were breweries still opening in the suburbs and beyond, including the game-changing Central City Brewers & Distillers of Surrey, but activity within the city limits was non-existent.

That all changed with a stroke of the legislative pen in 2013. A law was passed that allowed breweries to operate on-site taprooms, which made small operations more economically viable, and the largest city in British Columbia went from brewery wasteland to boomtown. Buoyed, too, by a general expansion in the beer offerings stocked by private liquor stores

Alibi Room

and shifting tastes in beer, Greater Vancouver began adding breweries on a remarkably regular basis, with almost 30 in operation as of the middle of 2017, according to the website *www.craftbeervancouver.ca*, and no doubt more in the planning. Almost all have taprooms as well.

Which means that beer-focused visitors have their work cut out. Even leaving aside such wonderful bars as the 50-tap **Alibi Room** and **Central City**'s outpost on Beatty Street, covering just the brewery "neighbourhoods" that have sprung up over the past few years – Brewery Creek to the

Storm Brewing

ADDRESS BOOK

ALIBI ROOM
157 Alexander Street, Vancouver, BC V6A 1B8
alibi.ca

◆

CENTRAL CITY BREWING
871 Beatty Street, Vancouver, BC V6B 2M6
centralcitybrewing.com

◆

33 ACRES BREWING COMPANY
15 West 8th Avenue, Vancouver, BC V5Y 1MB
33acresbrewing.com

◆

BRASSNECK BREWING
2148 Main Street, Vancouver, BC V5T 3C5
brassneck.ca

◆

STORM BREWING
310 Commercial Drive, Vancouver, BC V5L 1T1
stormbrewing.org

◆

PARALLEL 49 BREWING COMPANY
1950 Triumph Street, Vancouver, BC V5L 1K5
parallel49brewing.com

◆

POWELL BREWERY
1357 Powell Street, Vancouver, BC V5L 1G8
powellbeer.com

◆

DAGERAAD BREWING
#114, 3191 Thunderbird Crescent, Burnaby, BC V5A 3G1
dageraadbrewing.com

Parallel 49 Brewing

southeast of downtown and the Victoria Avenue-Powell Street area – will keep the beer traveller hopping.

Paring down the destinations isn't easy, either, but some highlights do stand out. Brewery Creek resident **33 Acres** is certainly worthy of a visit, as is nearby **Brassneck**, the latter operated by the same folk behind the Alibi Room. Eastside veteran **Storm Brewing** provides an always-entertaining and palate-enlightening anchor to the Powell-Victoria neighbourhood, with **Parallel 49** to the east, **Powell Brewery** to the west and several others

between and beyond. And for those willing to jump aboard the Skytrain, a five-minute walk from the Production Way station will bring you to one of the great up-and-comers of Canadian brewing, **Dageraad Brewing**.

All of which is, of course, merely the tip of a very sizeable iceberg, and one that looks destined to keep growing for some time to come.

HIGH STRENGTH WITH A VIEW

Many visitors to Vancouver will make the drive from the city to the celebrated ski hills at Whistler Mountain. Few will schedule a stop at the halfway point in Squamish, and that's a shame. A bedroom community for both Vancouver and Whistler, Squamish is an impressive destination in its own right, with climbing, hiking, fishing, kayaking and many other outdoor diversions, as well as a gorgeous mountain backdrop and surrounding wilderness. Plus, it is home to the **Howe Sound Inn & Brewing Company**.

For more than 20 years, Howe Sound has been serving a variety of ales and lagers at what is without question one of the country's most picturesque brewpubs, with soaring timbered ceilings and large windows that allow the majesty of the surrounding area to shine. The going was slow in the early days, the owners admit, but sped up considerably as the town's reputation as an outdoor sports enthusiast's paradise grew and regulations were redrawn allowing for brewpubs to sell their beer off-premises.

Whistler Mountain

ADDRESS BOOK

HOWE SOUND INN & BREWING COMPANY
37801 Cleveland Avenue, Squamish, BC V8B 0A7
howesound.com

Today, the original beer recipes crafted by founding brewer and BC craft beer pioneer John Mitchell have been supplemented by an impressive array of high-strength beers conceived by current brewer Franco Corno. Style purists might blanch at the thought of such beers as King Heffy, billed as an "Imperial Hefeweizen", or the 7.5% ABV Three Beavers Imperial Red Ale, but such potent brews number among the brewery's best work.

And if a day of outdoor activity followed by a night of strong ale leaves you feeling a bit, well, worn out, there is a bed awaiting your pleasure in one of the 20 comfortable rooms in the attached inn.

TORONTO BY BEER BARS

Toronto residents today have definite grounds to claim their home city as Canada's premier beer destination – although both Vancouverites and Montréalers have a basis for argument on that front. So impressive is the current Toronto beer scene, in fact, that it is challenging to identify just one place as its nucleus.

This was not always the case. Back in the days when Toronto could boast only a small fraction of the breweries that reside within its limits today, its chief claim to beer-soaked fame was its selection of beer bars, at the undisputed head of which was

WVRST

C'est What. Opened in 1988, the punning pub – *c'est* is a French contraction meaning "this is" but pronounced *say* – was by several years the first bar in the city to specialize in microbrewery beer. Transformed twice since then, first with an addition to the west, then a shift to the east, the original bar, complete with its craft-beer focus, has endured as a laudable drinking destination. The difference today is that it has company – a lot of company.

With the 2016 closing of Bar Volo (more about that later), the undisputed king – or, rather, kings – of Toronto beer bars are the Bar Hops. Born on King

Street, the original **Bar Hop** ascended the ranks quickly to become one of the city's top beer destinations. Rather than rest on these laurels, the owners then opened a second location up the road, adding a brewery to the 36 beers on tap and calling it **Bar Hop Brewco**. Together, not even a ten-minute walk apart, they are a formidable presence on the city's beer scene.

Furthermore, just a six-minute walk west of the King Street Bar Hop resides **WVRST**, which is what happens when you cross a Bavarian-style beer hall with a cool and hip craft-beer bar. Known for its excellent

C'est What

ADDRESS BOOK

C'EST WHAT
67 Front Street East at Church,
Toronto, ON M5E 1B5
cestwhat.com
◆

BAR HOP
391 King Street West, Toronto,
ON M5V 1K1
barhopbar.com
◆

BAR HOP BREWCO
137 Peter Street, Toronto,
ON M5V 2H3
barhopbar.com
◆

WVRST
609 King Street West, Toronto,
ON M5V 1M5
wvrst.com
◆

BIRRERIA VOLO
612 College Street, Toronto,
ON M6G 1B4
birreriavolo.com
◆

THE ONLY CAFE
972 Danforth Avenue, Toronto,
ON M4J 1L9
theonlycafe.com

A selection of bottled beers at WVRST.

sausages and constantly rotating two-dozen taps, WVRST adds to its presence on the local beer scene by being one of the few places in town to boast a vintage beer programme.

Slightly further away, in the middle of Little Italy, is **Birreria Volo**, offspring of the original Bar Volo, which closed and was levelled to make way for condominiums. A pioneer in Toronto for its large bottles-by-the-glass programme, which enables people to try revered and rare beers without footing the cost of the entire bottle, the new Volo also features 26 taps and a wide array of bottles, both cleverly assembled.

From that quintet, the field widens greatly with solid beer bars in the east, such as **The Only Cafe** and **Castro's Lounge**; **The Craft Brasserie & Grill** and **Bryden's** in the west; and Kensington Market's **Trinity Common** and the new and unrelated-to-the-Brasserie **CRAFT Beer Market** in between, among many others. All of which combine to cement the city's position as the nation's beer bar capital.

Above: Trinity Common. Top: Bar Hop Brewco.

ADDRESS BOOK

CASTRO'S LOUNGE
2116e Queen Street East, Toronto,
ON M4E 1E2
castroslounge.com
◆

**THE CRAFT BRASSERIE &
GRILL**
107 Atlantic Avenue,
Liberty Village, Toronto,
ON M6K 1Y2
thecraftbrasserie.com
◆

BRYDEN'S
2455 Bloor Street West, Toronto,
ON M6S 1P7
brydens.ca
◆

TRINITY COMMON
303 Augusta Avenue, Toronto,
ON M5T 2M2
trinitycommon.com
◆

CRAFT BEER MARKET
1 Adelaide Street East, Toronto,
ON M5C 2V9
craftbeermarket.ca

THREE DAYS
OF CASK-CONDITIONING

One of Canada's top beer events got its start on the patio of a now-defunct bar. It was perhaps an inauspicious start for **Cask Days**, but it spawned a festival that is likely to be the world's largest outside the UK that is entirely devoted to cask-conditioned ales.

Conceived in 2005 by publican Ralph Morana, the first Cask Days was little more than a modest collection of local cask-conditioned beers served on the patio of Bar Volo, for many years the city's top beer bar until its premises were purchased and demolished to make way for a condominium construction. Long before that ill-fated day, however, Cask Days had outgrown its modest beginnings and moved twice, eventually arriving at the redeveloped industrial site known as the Evergreen Brickworks. In 2013, what had been a Canadian breweries-only event added an international component with the importation of numerous casks from the UK. In 2014, a US state feature was added, with beers from California, and in 2016, the number of casks tapped topped 400 for the first time.

ADDRESS BOOK

CASK DAYS
*Evergreen Brickworks,
550 Bayview Avenue, Toronto,
ON M4W 3X8
festival.caskdays.com*

From its modest beginning with a mere 150 attendees, Cask Days has grown into a major event attracting thousands of visitors. It is held on the third weekend of October, with five tasting sessions spread over three days. Given the often difficult legal environment in which it functions, with Ontario beer laws sometimes resembling those of a bygone era, its success is both a testament to the perseverance of Morana and a triumph very much worth celebrating.

Pouring beer at Cask Days.

BICYCLING AMONG THE BREWERIES
(AND WINERIES)

Wineries and breweries happily coexist in Niagara.

ADDRESS BOOK

SILVERSMITH BREWING
1523 Niagara Stone Road,
Niagara-on-the-Lake,
ON LoS 1To
silversmithbrewing.com
◆

NIAGARA OAST HOUSE
BREWERS
2017 Niagara Stone Road,
Niagara-on-the-Lake,
ON LoS 1Jo
oasthousebrewers.com
◆

THE EXCHANGE BREWERY
7 Queen Street,
Niagara-on-the-Lake,
ON LoS 1Jo
exchangebrewery.com

While hardly as famous as the wine regions of France and Italy, southern Ontario boasts a robust viticulture industry on its Niagara Peninsula, stretching roughly from the city of Hamilton to Niagara Falls. More recently, that same district has become a bit of a beer region as well.

It only makes sense, really. Ask any winemaker and they will tell you that it takes a lot of good beer to make a great wine – a clear reference to the after-work imbibing habits of thirsty winery workers during harvest season. So why not keep the beer fresh by having the breweries close at hand?

As are most wine regions, Niagara is a fairly bucolic, agriculturally driven area with winding country roads and charming small towns and cities such as Beamsville and Niagara-on-the-Lake. Or, in other words, a region well suited to bicycle exploration. A good first stop for the cycling beer enthusiast is Silversmith Brewing, a brewery and modest beer hall built into a church that dates from 1890. Open from 10am daily, this accomplished young brewery not only boasts a laid-back taproom well suited to the early hours, but even produces a beer named

Bavarian Breakfast Wheat, not to mention an impressive Black Lager *schwarzbier* ideal for fuelling the ride ahead.

A scant few minutes down the road towards Niagara-on-the-Lake resides **Niagara Oast House Brewers** – longer, of course, if you want to get some cycling in first, perhaps via a diversion to the Konzelmann Estate Winery, near the shores of Lake Ontario. It is housed not in an actual oast house – traditionally the building in which hops were dried – but in a barn that suits the brewery objectives of what are often termed "farmhouse-style" beers, such as their peppery Saison and slightly nutty, sherry-evoking Bière de Garde. A most hospitable taproom and vineyard-adjacent terrace complete the picture.

The Exchange Brewery

After some further wine-country touring, perhaps taking in the Stratus or Marynissen wineries, it will be time to exchange bicycle tyres for shoe leather and park your ride in town, proceeding thereafter to the very young but thus far highly impressive **Exchange Brewery**. Housed on the main drag of Niagara-on-the-Lake, or NOTL as the town is informally known, The Exchange specializes in wood-conditioned beers, employing a brewer formerly of the similarly specialist Jolly Pumpkin Brewery across the border in Michigan to guide the way. And Sam Maxbauer has provided guidance in abundance, producing beers like the innocent-sounding but deliciously complex Golden Ale and musty, nutty and peppery Session Saison.

It's all enough to make you forget about your bicycle, and equally forget that most of the people you've passed on the road have been there for the wine rather than for the beer. Hard to imagine why, really.

The barrel room at The Exchange Brewery.

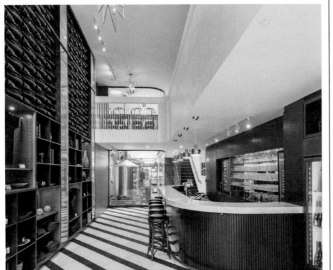

The Exchange Brewery's interior.

CAPITAL BEER

In the Ottawa of the early 2000s, a brewery crawl would not have required a massive amount of time. After the respectable **Clocktower Brew Pub**, one would swing quickly by the short-lived Abe & Roscoe's before being deeply disappointed by the offerings at the long-since-closed Master's Brew Pub & Brasserie. Then, nothing. This sad state of affairs continued more or less through the first decade of this new millennium, the players changing but growing and improving little (save for the Clocktower, it needs to be noted, which has endured,

expanded and improved). Then, at the end of 2010, contract brewer **Kichesippi** bought out the brewery where its beer was being made and things began to change.

As Kichesippi sorted out its new life, bringing in veteran brewer Don Harms and adding a stellar Heller Highwater lager to its line-up, among other moves, **Big Rig Brewery** came to town with, first, a brewpub, then a production brewery and, finally, another pub. Others soon followed, including **Dominion City Brewing** near to where Heritage once brewed, and the hobby brewery turned growing business, **Beyond the Pale**. Along the way, the National Capital Region developed one of the best brewery walks in eastern Canada.

Begin at **Tooth and Nail Brewing**, an up-and-comer *par excellence*, where Thursday through Sunday the taps open at noon. In a stylish and sleek taproom, enjoy one of Canada's best first-of-the-day beers in the form of Vim & Vigor Pilsner alongside a charcuterie and cheese or veggies and dip board, perhaps with a Tenacity Pale Ale to follow before walking the ten minutes to Beyond the Pale.

Kichesippi Beer

As of mid-2017, the taproom at Beyond the Pale was still in development, but the somewhat industrial brewery founded by two childhood friends still had much to recommend it. Such as Aromatherapy, a massively aromatic IPA that will appeal even to those who typically dislike the style, and eight oft-changing taps, featuring recipes culled from a catalogue of over 160 beers and counting.

Next on the list, and almost certainly one of Canada's most atmospheric breweries,

Samples at Les Brasseurs du Temps.

The atmospheric terrace at Les Brasseurs du Temps.

is **Les Brasseurs du Temps** across the river in Québec. It's only a few minutes from downtown, but closer to 45 minutes walking from Beyond the Pale, meaning you'll have time to develop a thirst for a refreshing, drily malty ESB 1821. As night falls, Les Brasseurs du Temps only grows prettier, so hang around for dinner and, since your exercise for the day is done, a few of the brewery's stronger beers, such as the marvellously fruity-spicy and warming Trois Portages Tripel. Sightseeing in the nation's capital, after all, can wait for another day.

ADDRESS BOOK

CLOCKTOWER BREW PUB
575 Bank Street, Ottawa, ON
K1S 5L7 (and other locations)
clocktower.ca
◆

KICHESIPPI BEER
866 Campbell Avenue, Ottawa,
ON K2A 2C5
kbeer.ca
◆

BIG RIG KITCHEN & BREWERY
2750 Iris Street, Ottawa,
ON K2C 3C9
bigrigbrew.com
◆

DOMINION CITY BREWING
15–5510 Canotek Road,
Gloucester, ON K1J 9J4
dominioncity.ca
◆

BEYOND THE PALE BREWERY
250 City Centre Avenue,
Bay 106, Ottawa, ON K1R 6K7
beyondthepale.ca
◆

TOOTH AND NAIL BREWING
3 Irving Avenue, Ottawa,
ON K1Y 1Z2
toothandnailbeer.com
◆

LES BRASSEURS DU TEMPS
170 rue Montcalm, Gatineau,
Québec, QC J8X 2M2
brasseursdutemps.com

QUÉBÉCOIS CREATIVITY
IN MONTRÉAL

Le Saint-Bock

L'Amere a Boire

T he province of Québec was notoriously late to the microbrewing party. Its first two breweries not named Molson or Labatt opened in 1986: two years after neighbouring Ontario got its start and four years behind the pioneering Canadian province of British Columbia. Even after things picked up in the 1990s, progress in *la belle province* was slow and sporadic, with breweries opening and closing with almost equal regularity.

Still, some stuck. Les Brasseurs du Nord, better known by its brand name of Boréale, made an impact with a beer called Rousse, setting the stage for numerous others of the same flavourful ilk. McAuslan Brewing established a distinctly Québéc style of pale ale with St Ambroise Pale Ale and created a market for stouts with St Ambroise Oatmeal Stout. And a brewery on Montréal's south shore called Unibroue set the stage for Belgian-inspired beers in the province.

All of which brings us to the 21st century and the city of Montréal's blossoming as a Canadian centre for craft-brewing excellence. The Québec brewery name most familiar to those outside the province, aside from Maudite and Fin du Monde creator Unibroue, is likely **Dieu du Ciel!**, and while the brewery has moved its bottle and keg production north of the city, the original Montréal brewpub remains a much recommended destination for beer-interested visitors. The heartland of that city's beer scene, however, resides at the meeting of Rue Ontario and St-Denis.

There, within a meandering stroll that tops out at Rue Sherbrooke and ventures east to near Avenue Papineau, you will find the city's original and still justly well-regarded brewpub,

Above and top: Bénélux

Le Cheval Blanc, the beer bar-cum-brewpub **Le Saint-Bock**, Czech beer style specialist **L'Amère à Boire**, the ever-increasingly impressive brewpub **Bénélux**, and the city tap of *saison* specialist Hopfenstark, **Station Ho.st**. Add in beer and whisky bar **Pub L'Île Noire** and you have the makings of a very fine walk indeed.

ADDRESS BOOK

DIEU DU CIEL!
29 Laurier West, Montréal,
QC H2T 2N2
dieuduciel.com
◆

LE CHEVAL BLANC
809 rue Ontario Est, Montréal,
QC H2L 1P1
lechevalblanc.ca
◆

LE SAINT-BOCK
1749 rue Saint-Denis, Montréal,
QC H2X 3K4
saintbock.com
◆

L'AMÈRE À BOIRE
2049 rue Saint-Denis, Montréal,
QC H2X 3K8
amereaboire.com
◆

BÉNÉLUX
245 rue Sherbrooke Ouest,
Montréal, QC H2X 1X7
brasseriebenelux.com/sherbrooke
◆

STATION HO.ST
1494 Ontario Street E, Montréal,
QC H2L 1S3
stationhost.ca
◆

PUB L'ÎLE NOIRE
1649 rue Saint-Denis, Montréal,
QC H2X 3K4
ilenoire.com

NEW BEER
IN THE OLD CITY

The provincial capital of Québec has much to recommend it, from a world-famous winter carnival to its gorgeous UNESCO World Heritage-protected Old City and the nearby Montmorency Falls. Up until recently, however, it didn't have a lot to offer the beer traveller.

As with many North American cities, the craft-beer-challenged nature of Québec City began to change as the first decade of the 21st century gave way to the second. From a pair of breweries – **la Barberie** and **l'Inox**, the latter the original city brewpub dating from 1987 and relocated to the Grande Allée a decade ago – the capital greatly expanded to well over a dozen, and to its single, atmospheric but not terribly imaginative beer-focused pub it added several others, including the laudable **Bateau de Nuit**. And along the way it became home to the **Festibière du Québec**.

Founded in 2010 and run in mid-August, when the local weather is usually at its best, the festival has a location that should be the envy of every arena or conference hall beer festival

The Montmorency Falls, near Quebec City.

the world over: on the old port lands with the city fortifications as a backdrop. It runs for four days and, as with most such popular festivals, the best time for visitors to plan their tasting is before work lets out on the Thursday or Friday.

That said, as there is no admission – once you purchase your tasting glass you can feel free to come and go as you wish – it is possible to conduct more studious sampling during the day and return at night or over the weekend for the entertainment. It is a festival that can get crowded, particularly in the tents where the beer is being poured, but seldom or never does it lose its laid-back appeal.

As for the beer, most of the attending breweries are from Québec, so if you're unfamiliar with the local beer scene, there will be much to discover. And when you're done tasting, or merely wish to take a break from it all, the surrounding city offers an experience as close to France as you can get without leaving North America.

WHILE YOU'RE THERE
If your visit to Québec doesn't coincide exactly with the Festibière, visit **La Cour Arrière Festibière**, an outdoor "pop-up" patio with 26 taps and exclusive and limited-edition beers, that runs from mid-summer into the early fall.

ADDRESS BOOK

LA BARBERIE
310 rue Saint-Roch, Québec,
QC G1K 6S2
labarberie.com
◆

L'INOX
655 Grande Allée Est, Québec,
QC G1R 2K4
brasserieinox.com
◆

BATEAU DE NUIT
275 rue Saint-Jean, Québec,
QC G1R 1N8
◆

FESTIBIÈRE DU QUÉBEC
Espace 400e,
100 Quai Saint-André, Québec,
QC G1K 3Y2
infofestibiere.com
◆

LA COUR ARRIÈRE
FESTIBIÈRE
Port du Québec, 84 rue Dalhousie,
Québec, QC G1K 8M5
infofestibiere.com

Above and top: La Barberie

FUCK
ALEXANDER KEITH

The infamous IPA-that-isn't-really-an-IPA.

Beer in Halifax has a long, long history, and one aspect of that history will be almost drummed into your head if you are a traveller visiting the city. That aspect is Alexander Keith.

Keith was a real person and he brewed beer – of that there is no doubt. But today his name is attached to a beer brewed by the Anheuser-Busch-InBev-owned Labatt Breweries, which in blind tastings is all but identical to the host of mainstream lagers that crowd maritime beer store shelves. Doubling that sin is the fact that said beer is identified as an India pale ale.

Well, to hell with that.

Or, as the duo behind **Unfiltered Brewing** in the city's north end might put it, fuck that. Because to Greg Nash and Andrew Murphy – whose chosen URL for their brewery is unfuckingfiltered.com – the proof is in the pint glass. In contrast to the mild manner of Alexander Keith India Pale Ale, there is nothing restrained or understated about the Unfiltered beers, with even the brewery's gluten-reduced options offering bold and uncompromising

flavours and bitterness. Mainstay beer Twelve Years to Zion is itself worth the trip to Halifax and also a statement of brewer Nash's long journey to having his own brewery, rich as it is in peachy fruit, balanced, citrusy bitterness and warming strength. Softer Exile on North Street is a gluten-reduced IPA that nonetheless convinces with a sticky malt body and citrus-zesty finish. The taproom bar may not necessarily be the finest in all of Halifax, but the beer selection will keep you in your seat for a good while.

And if it doesn't, just up the road is **Good Robot**, a hipper, slightly contrived-feeling brewery tap that nevertheless boasts an appealing house-party vibe, even on a Saturday afternoon. Complementing the atmosphere are such brews as the superbly named, blackcurrant-y stout Tom Waits for No One, and the dryly caramelly lager Xtra Big Ass.

After all of which you may still find yourself tempted to take the tour of the ersatz Keith's brewery that Labatt has staged in the heart of downtown. Just don't be surprised if you emerge from the experience thinking, "Well, fuck that."

ADDRESS BOOK

UNFILTERED BREWING
6041 North Street, Halifax,
NS B3K 1P1
unfuckingfiltered.com
◆

GOOD ROBOT BREWING
2736 Robie Street, Halifax,
NS B3K 4P2
goodrobotbrewing.ca
◆

THE HENRY HOUSE
1222 Barrington Street, Halifax,
NS B3J 1Y4
henryhouse.ca

Good Robot Brewing

WHILE YOU'RE THERE

No visit to Halifax would be complete without at least a pint at **The Henry House**, now a pub housed in a historic venue but once the home of the Granite Brewery, Nova Scotia's first modern craft brewery. The Granite's very fine Best Bitter is still poured, usually as a dry-hopped and cask-conditioned ale, and remains highly recommended.

THE REST OF THE WORLD

THE OTHER
OKTOBERFEST

If someone set you down unaware in the centre of Blumenau, a city in the southern Brazilian state of Santa Catarina, you might think you had just been transported to Germany. From the Alpine architecture to the Bavarian-influenced cuisine, it's about as far from the stereotypically Brazilian Carnival and beach scenes as you can get.

That's attributable to the city's long German history, which stretches all the way back to its founding. In 1850, immigrant Hermann Bruno Otto Blumenau, along with 17 other settlers, arrived from Germany to form a colony that lasted until the Brazilian government assumed control of the growing habitation a decade later. Even then, Blumenau remained the official director of the village and was

responsible for the development of schools and hospitals to serve the emergent community.

The legacy of that German heritage has had much impact on the life and development of this city of 300,000-plus, not least of which has been the establishment of one of the world's largest Oktoberfests held outside of Munich. (There is some dispute as to whether the **Blumenau Oktoberfest**

Celebrating during the parade to Oktoberfest.

Above and left: Oktoberfest in Blumenau.

ADDRESS BOOK

OKTOBERFEST BLUMENAU
*Parque Vila Germânica,
Rua Alberto Stein 199, Velha,
Blumenau, SC 89036-200
oktoberfestblumenau.com.br*
◆

BASEMENT ENGLISH PUB
*Rua Paul Hering 35,
Blumenau, SC 89010-050
basementpub.com.br*

or the Kitchener-Waterloo Oktoberfest in Ontario, Canada, is second to Munich. I shall not weigh in on the subject, except to note that my personal preference is for the Brazilian.)

Unlike Munich's Oktoberfest, Blumenau's event takes place entirely within the month of October, running daily for two and a half weeks at the Parque Vila Germânica, or German Village Park, located just outside of town. For the duration of Oktoberfest, the park transforms into a village of its own, with large music halls, outdoor beer gardens for when the weather cooperates and, of course, plenty of beer from local favourite, the Heineken-owned Eisenbahn, as well as other craft breweries, mostly from neighouring areas.

Smaller than the Munich original, yet still large enough to be considered a massive event, the Blumenau Oktoberfest is a useful counterpoint to the German original, half beer festival and half rollicking civic party. And it is an excellent excuse to explore a fascinating and undertravelled part of South America.

WHILE YOU'RE THERE
Having long since sold the Eisenbahn brewery, the founding family has gone on to establish the town's top beer bar, the **Basement English Pub**. While the beer list tilts strongly toward the brewery they once owned and operated, there is still plenty from elsewhere in Brazil to keep a beer taster occupied.

THE HEART OF
BRAZILIAN BEER

Prior to Brazil's hosting of the World Cup in 2014, it is unlikely than many people outside South America had heard of Curitiba. Which really reflects how little people from beyond that continent generally know about Brazil, since Curitiba is not only a large city of close to two million people, but also, pertinent to those with an interest in beer, it is fast developing into the hub of Brazilian craft brewing.

One reason for this is Cervejaria Bodebrown, founded and led by brewer and brewing educator Samuel Christophe Cavalcanti Cabral. Not content with merely running what is, in Brazilian craft-beer terms, a fair-sized operation, Cabral also operates a brewing school in Curitiba, at which he has trained numerous now-successful fellow brewers. His brewery, meanwhile, continues to be one of the most influential in the country, with beers such as the passion-fruity Perigosa, originally brewed as Brazil's first double-IPA, and the spicy, Scottish-style Wee Heavy. Currently in the process of financing a large expansion,

ADDRESS BOOK

CERVEJARIA BODEBROWN
*Rua Carlos de Laet 1015 - Hauer,
Curitiba, PR 81610-050
novafabrica.bodebrown.com.br*
◆

WAY BEER
*Rua Pérola 331 - Pinhais,
PR 83325-200
waybeer.com.br*
◆

GAUDEN BIER
*Avenida Manoel Ribas 7015 -
Santa Felicidade,
Curitiba, PR 82320-060
gaudenbier.com.br*
◆

CLUBE DO MALTE
*Rua Desembargador Motta,
2200, Curitiba, PR 80510-170
clubedomalte.com.br/bar*

Bodebrown operates a shop at the brewery but unfortunately does not at present run a tasting room, although its beers are widely available in town.

A differently influential brewery sits just outside of town: **Way Beer**. Among the first to use Amazonian wood to flavour its beer, by aging its strong Amburana Lager to a deliciously cinnamony spiciness in amburana wood, Way also became, in the early 2010s, one of the first Brazilian breweries to experiment with mixed fermentation. Those beers, dubbed the Sour Me Not line, also draw from the Amazon in the form of the fruits used to flavour them. Way runs regular open houses at the brewery, where tours are offered and all its beers are available for purchase.

Curitiba is also home to unusual brewing relationships, such as the one that sees **Gauden Bier** share its brewery with smaller firms like the impressive Morada Cia Etílica, DUM Cervejaria, brewer of the excellent Petroleum Imperial Stout, and the improbably named F#%*ing Beer. It's a relationship that is more than a simple contract brewing

Curitiba city centre

arrangement, since the principals of all three smaller enterprises have a regular presence at the brewery, yet not quite an equal partnership. And it works.

To sample the wares of these and other Curitiba breweries, including Way Beer neighbour Bastards Brewing and newcomer Cervejaria Swamp, pay a visit to **Clube do Malte**, the city's leading beer bar, with one location in the centre of the city and another slightly northeast of downtown.

A BAR CALLED
FRANGÓ

When asked to name my favourite bars around the world, a handful of very special places spring to mind, all of which are documented within these pages. The one that regularly surprises people, however, is a bar of which very few people outside South America have heard, even if among that continent's beer cognoscenti it is the stuff of legend. It is a bar in São Paulo, Brazil. A bar called .

When first I visited São Paulo, it struck me as the most intimidating city I had ever visited, and I say that as a committed big-city resident and ardent urban explorer. The sheer size and scope of the place was stunning, well illustrated by the view from the roof of my hotel, which in every direction revealed buildings and masses of people. At street level, it seemed as impersonal a city as I had ever visited.

Yet that all ended the moment I stepped into FrangÓ. If you go no further than just inside the door of this beer bar in the northwest of the city, named after the Portuguese word for

ADDRESS BOOK

FRANGÓ
Largo da Matriz Nossa Senhora do Ó, 168 - Freguesia do Ó, São Paulo, SP 02925-040
frangobar.com.br

"chicken" with the Ó capitalized in reference to the street on which it is found, you might think it no more than a small and inviting bar with an impressive beer list. And you would be quite right, except for the "small" part. For in addition to having one of the country's finest beer lists, if not *the finest*, and uniformly impressive bar snacks (including the famously delicious chicken croquettes, known as *coxinha*), FrangÓ also rambles, first down a narrow hallway to a more open area in the back, then down the stairs to an expansive lower floor. Along the way you will encounter walls clad in various pieces of brewery memorabilia and brewery posters, domestic kitchen-style tables and chairs, refrigerators packed with beers from across the country and around the world, and crowds of smiling people drinking those beers and enjoying themselves.

No matter where you station yourself in this wonderful bar, though, such is the atmosphere and greeting that you will almost certainly find yourself feeling as if you've just arrived home. Even if it's your first time in Brazil and you speak not a single word of Portuguese.

85

MEXICAN BEER,
NO LIME REQUIRED

There are worse places to find yourself in November than Mexico City. Sure, the weather can be variable, but at least it is guaranteed to be warmer than Toronto, London or Seattle. And notwithstanding my few wet nights there, generally drier, too. Plus, there is beer. A considerable amount of beer, in fact, in the form of Cerveza México, a three-day exhibition of the best of Mexican craft beer.

Held at the Pepsi Center at the World Trade Center, Cerveza México is the premier showcase for Mexican brewers, put on in conjunction with the country's top beer competition and, for professional and would-be pro brewers, a trade conference as well. To get a figurative and literal taste of what is arguably the most exciting developing beer culture in the Americas, there is nowhere better.

The format of the festival will be familiar to anyone who has been to national-showcase beer fests: a multitude of brewery booths scattered around a display space of 4,800 sq m (almost 52,000 sq ft), with samples to taste and crowds to

Cerveza México

ADDRESS BOOK

CERVEZA MÉXICO
*Pepsi Center, Calle Dakota S/N,
Colonia Nápoles, Del. Benito
Juárez, 03810 Mexico City
tradex.mx/cerveza*

navigate. Except that Mexico being a younger craft-beer market than, say, the United States, the crowds aren't quite so dense, and the chances of finding a brewer or brewery owner at their booth are much higher.

Mexico has a rapidly evolving brewing culture, and wise visiting tasters will seek out the unusual and unconventional, such as the Mexican Imperial stout the country is on the verge of claiming as its national style, flavoured with mole spices. Or you could try the local takes on traditional beers, like Chaneque's Mezcal IPA, aged in tequila and mezcal barrels.

With ten hours of sampling available on Friday and Saturday – afternoon entry on Friday is strongly recommended – plus another seven hours on Sunday, there is no reason that this one weekend can't give you a great overview of a tremendous beer market. And leave you planning your next beer trip to Guatemala, or Cancún, or Baja California, or even back to Mexico City.

BEER TASTING IN
PARADISE

When I first went to the area of Mexico near Cancún known as the Riviera Maya, the last thing I expected to find was craft beer. And I didn't. Mind you, as I was there to get married and never left the resort where our wedding was held, that was kind of to be expected. Things were quite different a few years later, however, when I returned on a specific mission to discover Mexican craft beer.

On that trip, my destination resort was the **Fairmont Mayakoba**, at the time and, to my knowledge, still today the only resort in the region both to stock craft beer and employ a qualified individual to oversee it. Back then, that employee was Luis Garcés, an up-and-coming junior manager and certified Cicerone who assisted me in assembling the largest-collection possible of beers from the still-emerging Mexican craft-beer segment, all of which we tasted over the course of several days.

One night, after we had finished our sampling, Luis escorted my wife and me off the resort and into Playa del Carmen, the main coastal city south of Cancún. After enjoying dinner on the commercial strip known simply as "the Fifth", we made our way down the road

Sunset at the beach in Playa del Carmen.

Club de la Cerveza

to a bar then still far enough removed from the madness of the touristy area that it was refreshingly quiet, though by no means deserted. That bar was **Club de la Cerveza**, and every time Maggie and I have travelled to the Riviera Maya since, we have made a point of paying it a visit.

Owned and operated by expat Argentinean Miguel Antoniucci, Club de la Cerveza has notably improved on every visit – not that it was all that shabby to begin with. Open to the night air and with more tables outside than in, it's a bar that would charm even if it offered only a handful of halfway-decent beers, much less the more than

respectable selection of local, national and international brews that Miguel goes to great lengths to stock. Add in a fully stocked bar and smiling, English-speaking staff and you have an equation that makes Club de la Cerveza a required stop for anyone visiting the area, beer aficionado or not!

ADDRESS BOOK

FAIRMONT MAYAKOBA
Carretera Federal Cancún,
Playa del Carmen Km. 298,
Riviera Maya,
Quintana Roo, 77710
fairmont.com/mayakoba-riviera-maya

CLUB DE LA CERVEZA
5 Avenida Norte entre calles
34 y 38 Norte, Xaman-Ha,
Playa del Carmen, 77710
clubdelacerveza.mx

DRINKING IN OLD SAN JUAN

Many casual travellers to Puerto Rico's capital city will focus their explorations on the south side of historic Old San Juan. In fact, if they arrive by cruise ship, as do two million visitors each year, they are unlikely to get much beyond the middle of the picturesque cobblestoned city, given the combined deterrents of a steep hill, dense crowds and plenty to see and do within a few blocks of the cruise-ship port. That would, however, mean missing one of the Caribbean's most charming beer bars.

Almost as far away from the cruise-ship docks as it is possible to get without leaving the old city, La Taberna Lúpulo is still not more than a 20-minute walk from the terminal, and well worth the stroll. Open to the street on two sides and boasting the sort of laid-back ambience one only finds in tropical climates, behind its yellow stone exterior the bar boasts high, timbered ceilings with hanging fans, well-trodden floors and 50 taps plus 150 bottles of ales and lagers.

While Puerto Rican craft brews are found on tap and in the bottle, the industry is still struggling to find its way, so pride of place is instead bestowed upon well-known craft beers from the continental US, of which Puerto Rico is, of course, a part, including regular offerings from Stone, Abita, Founders and Bell's. A handful of European beers, including the excellent and hot-climate-friendly Weihenstephaner Weissbier, complete the draught selection.

Perhaps it was the enchanting nature of Old San Juan or the history that permeates every wall, floorboard or cobblestone in the city, but being at Taberna Lúpulo reminds me of nothing so much as drinking in one of the endearingly rundown bars of the French Quarter of New Orleans, except without the decrepitude and with much, much better beer. My first visit lasted no longer than a few hours, but the draw of the bar was sufficiently strong that, even as I was saying my goodbyes, I somehow knew that I'd be returning soon.

ADDRESS BOOK

LA TABERNA LÚPULO
151 Calle San Sebastián,
San Juan, 00901
latabernalupulo.com

La Taberna Lúpulo

The bar at La Taberna Lúpulo.

GROWING EXCITEMENT IN CHILE

When Tim Webb and I were putting together the first edition of *The World Atlas of Beer* in 2012, it was my task to sort through the Americas, including Latin America. I was quickly able to determine that Brazil was the regional leader, Argentina placed second in terms of the craft-brewing development and Chile came in third.

Things have changed since. From almost nowhere, Mexico has stepped up to assume the second position, and while Argentinean beer was stalled for a few years, Chile set off in pursuit of craft beer success at a dead run, bringing itself firmly into third place. Nowhere is this more apparent than in the capital of Santiago.

With almost one-third of the nation's population within its metropolitan boundaries, Santiago's sprawling nature makes having a central base for your explorations a must, and in that role I recommend Barrio Lastarria. First settled in the 1500s, the district is today home to a mix of residents and a dense concentration of bars, cafés and restaurants.

Unfortunately, none of those bars or restaurants are specifically beer specialists, although even a little *sanguchería*, or sandwich shop, such as **José Ramón 277**, will stock a selection of regional craft brews on tap. The neighbourhood does, however, provide easy reach to the city's best beer spots.

One such example is the **Barbudo Beer Garden**, a taxi ride away in the Villa Seca neighbourhood, but well worth the trip for its 15 taps of mostly local beers – a high number for Santiago! – and large garden in the back or the cosy upstairs

for when the weather is less cooperative. A bit closer in the opposite direction is **Loom Brewing**, a modestly sized brewpub that also functions as a Chile-focused beer bar, with its own brews normally occupying only two or three of the seven taps.

For beer-cuisine fans, **Mossto** is a bar and restaurant where almost everything on the menu contains a beery element of some sort. Although the beer selection is modest, with a dozen taps pouring a mix of Mossto's own and guest beers, plus a good selection of

José Ramon 277

ADDRESS BOOK

JOSÉ RAMÓN 277
José Ramón Gutiérrez 277,
Barrio Lastarria, Santiago,
8320162

◆

BARBUDO BEER GARDEN
Jorge Washington 176,
Plaza Ñuñoa, Santiago, 7790827
barbudo.cl

◆

LOOM BREWING
Bellavista 0360, Providencia,
Santiago, 7530192
loom.cl

◆

MOSSTO CRAFT BEER & BREW
FOOD
Avenida Condell 1460,
Providencia, Santiago, 7501463
mossto.cl

Loom Brewing

imported bottles, it's the sort of place where you read the owners' claim that their team is working to grow Chilean beer culture and you're inclined to believe it.

Given the enthusiasm of the Chilean public for craft beer, places like these are likely harbingers of a greater scene to come. Having tasted the beers of more mature breweries such as Tübinger and Kross and those of such young up-and-comers as Jester and Emperador, I have little doubt that Chilean brewers are up to the task of speeding that development along.

Ushuaia at night.

ALE AT THE END OF THE WORLD

BY TIM WEBB

Nobody goes to Tierra del Fuego, "the land of fire", for the beer, but the fact that craft brewing has reached here is extraordinary. The southern tip of the Americas is not a destination in the literal sense, despite being branded *Il Fin del Mundo* ("the end of the world") by its tourist people. The port town of Ushuaia, sheltered from the Southern Ocean by the Beagle Strait, is more a stopping-off point for liners cruising between Valparaiso and Buenos Aires, or for those embarking on the hardiest ships of all to Antarctica.

Take the narrow-gauge railway up to the disused mine and you've done the tourism bit, beyond the strange joy of just being in a place where the weather hones survivors, not sun-loving party people. Drinkers in weatherproof capes cluster among ropes and pulleys off salt-encrusted rigging, in bars that keep them warm with hearty stews.

At the **Fuegian Beverage Company**, also known as Cervecería Beagle, the world's southernmost brewery, the challenges are different from elsewhere. The peninsula may be contiguous with the continental landmass, but all supplies arrive by ship from Buenos Aires, four days and more than 3,000km (almost 2,000 miles) away, with the risk that en route they were parboiled in the hold of a freighter or grilled on some tropical quayside.

The kegs were left behind by former suppliers, or were else adapted by taking an oxyacetylene torch to the fittings of outmoded soft-drink containers. When the supply line for CO_2 cylinders failed a while back, the Fuegian Peninsula became the only place in Christendom to have no draught beer for nearly a month. With beer bottling all done by hand, the additional labour involved in doubling its output played havoc with staff morale – and overtime.

Their joke that the brewery is held together with wire is only half-affectionate. Throughout the five-month-long tourist season, demand outstrips production. To brew here is to be dedicated.

WHILE YOU'RE THERE

In Ushuaia, the **Dublin** is the top beer venue, or try **El Viejo Marino** if you want a giant spider crab alongside.

ADDRESS BOOK

FUEGIAN BEVERAGE COMPANY
Heroes de Malvinas 4160, Ushuaia, Tierra del Fuego
◆

DUBLIN
9 de Julio 168, Ushuaia, Tierra del Fuego, V9410DDD
◆

EL VIEJO MARINO
Calle Maipu 229, Ushuaia, Tierra del Fuego, V9410BJE

SIPPING BEER
BY THE ANDES

In contrast to most countries with craft-beer cultures, small-scale brewing in Argentina first took hold most firmly not in the country's large urban areas, but in the achingly beautiful Lake District of northern Patagonia. Specifically, as breweries came and went in and around Buenos Aires, a couple of dozen could be reliably found in the region anchored by the cities of El Bolsón to the south and San Carlos de Bariloche to the north.

It is perhaps not as surprising a development as it might seem. The district was home to a community of German

Cerveza Artesanal Blest

Julio Migoya, founder of Cerveza Artesanal Blest.

immigrants as long ago as the mid-to-late 19th century and is today the heart of the Argentinean hop-growing industry, so you could say that a love of beer is pretty much impregnated into the community's DNA.

There are numerous breweries scattered between and around the two cities, including **Cervecería Lowther**, the most central brewery in Bariloche, and the well-regarded **Blest**, credited by many as Argentina's first brewpub. For festival-goers, this area offers two main events: the Festival Cosecha de Lúpulo, or hop-harvest festival, each

February in El Bolsón, and the Fiesta de la Cerveza Artesanal in Bariloche each December.

Whether in the area for a festival or not, one place you won't want to miss is **Cerveza Berlina**, one of the largest breweries in the region, but also one of the best. While the company has grown greatly in recent years, with five bars now open in Buenos Aires and one in Rosario, the original brewery restaurant and pub retains an endearing, rustic appeal with its corrugated-steel bar-front, weathered furnishings and jumbled décor accented by dried hop vines. Beers offer something

Cervecería Lowther

to please almost everyone, from a Patagonia Special Bitter made with hops harvested in El Bolsón to a viscously malty Old Ale.

The best reason to make the trip to where Berlina began, however, is the vista on display from the patio, which affords a spectacular view of the Andes mountains. Sat back on a sunny day with a pint of IPA, you begin to understand why a trio of brewing brothers might have been moved to base their fledgling operation here rather than in crowded, sometimes chaotic Buenos Aires. And at that moment, you will be very thankful they did.

BREWING AMERICAN ALES
THE JAPANESE WAY

C raft beer in Japan has had a bit of a rocky history. First, it was effectively illegal: a law mandated that a brewery be able to produce a minimum of 2 million litres (almost 530,000 US gallons) of beer from the outset – a virtual impossibility for a small start-up business. Then, once that number was rolled back to 60,000 litres (almost 16,000 US gallons) in the mid-1990s, there followed a wave of brewery openings. Almost inevitably, after so many breweries opened in a country with no great beer culture, a

great many closed. But one was biding its time until the situation seemed right. That was **Baird Brewing**.

Living in Japan and working in an office at the time of the change in law, American expat Bryan Baird saw potential in the new Japanese beer market. So much so that he returned to the United States in 1997 to train and apprentice as a brewer before returning to Japan to begin planning his brewery with his wife, Sayuri. It was the summer of 2000 before they finally opened their taproom, and the end of the year before Japanese bureaucracy finally allowed them

Baird Brewing

to begin selling their own beers. Since then, Baird Brewing has gone on to be not just one of the great survivors among Japanese craft breweries, but also one of the largest and very best.

Baird now operates six taprooms and beer gardens in Tokyo and slightly beyond. The newest addition to the family is the **Takadanobaba Taproom**, opened in the spring of 2016 and featuring *kushiage*, or fried meat and vegetable skewers, but the jewel in the crown is the **Brewery Gardens Shuzenji**, an indoor-outdoor space located on the third floor of the company's production brewery, which

Baird Takadanobaba Taproom

Baird Taproom Nakameguro

opened in 2014. With a stunning view of the surrounding area, it is indeed a place to experience.

That said, Shuzenji is three hours from central Tokyo, and the original Baird pub at **Numazu Fishmarket** is almost as far. Which makes a visit to the brewery's first Tokyo digs, **Baird Taproom Nakameguro**, which opened in the spring of 2008 all that more appealing.

It's admittedly not the most "Japanese" place, with a menu focus on pizzas, but with 26 taps it is one of the best in the Baird family for sampling a variety of the brewery's beers. Unusual domestic and imported guest beers are also included, as are cask-conditioned ales. However, the highlight here is definitely all things Baird Brewing, from the year-round Wabi-Sabi Japan Pale Ale to the mandarin orange-enhanced Natsumikan Summer Ale.

It shouldn't take more than an hour or two for you to understand why Baird is the respected Japanese beer pioneer it is today.

EARLY RUMBLINGS
IN BEIJING

Contrary to popular belief, brewing did not come only just recently to Beijing. For after such pioneering German-origin breweries and beer gardens as the **Paulaner Bräuhaus Beijing**, which opened in 1992, a number of Chinese-owned and operated imitators followed, giving the Chinese capital a modest assortment of largely lager-producing breweries scattered within its borders. The problem was, German originals aside, most of them weren't very good.

Fast-forward, then, to October 2010 and the opening of **Great Leap Brewing**, Beijing's first modern craft brewery, and the series of other openings it has since spawned. Now operating in three locations, Great Leap quickly developed a following among mostly expat Westerners thirsty for something other than a light-tasting lager. Success necessitated expansion, and a mere three years later a second location was opened, then later a third, allowing the company to expand greatly the range of styles produced, which today includes flagship Little General IPA, seasoned entirely with Chinese Qingdao Flower hops.

Above and top: Great Leap Brewing

Slow Boat Brewery

Others soon followed Great Leap's lead. **Slow Boat Brewery** opened in 2011, and although the production facility is situated within sight of the Great Wall, the company also operates a brewpub in the Sanlitun District of the city. (The original Beijing taproom closed in 2017 due to "architectural violations" in the building above. It is not known at the time of writing if it will reopen.) All I sampled from the four-year-old operation was balanced and refreshingly well attenuated, whether a Vienna lager like the slightly earthy Endeavour or the flagship Monkey's Fist IPA, the best of that style I tasted in Beijing.

More recent arrivals include **Jing-A**, where obvious attempts have been made to embrace a Chinese approach to brewing, with rice, ginger and wasabi appearing in the lightly sweet and spicy Koji Red Ale, Sichuan

Beer sampler at Jing-A.

Jing-A

pepper and osmanthus flower in the floral and off-dry Full Moon Farmhouse Ale and, most interestingly of all, a strong, experimental ale partially fermented by the wild baijiu yeast known as *jiuqu*. The Chinese-owned **NBeer**, a popular brewpub that is hip in a sort of funky, punk rock kind of way, perhaps curiously expends little effort in exploring uniquely Chinese approaches to brewing.

And final among the principal five Beijing breweries is **Panda Brew**, catching my attention almost immediately with its Kuding Pale Ale, which employs Chinese herbs as well as hops for bittering, producing a fascinating and unique bitterness quite unlike that of a purely hopped beer, making it perhaps a harbinger of Chinese beers to come.

HITTING THE HAWKER STALLS
IN SINGAPORE

93

Anyone who has spent time in Southeast Asia will understand that street food and hawker stalls are far removed from the takeouts and food courts of the West. As much as we may now glorify our food trucks and "must-try" kiosks in North America and parts of Europe, Asian street and stall food is of a different class altogether.

What is widely lacking from the Asian hawker-stall food experience, however, is good beer. Sure, you can usually find a Singha to go with your *gai bing* in Bangkok or an Angkor Premium to wash down your *fish amok* in Phnom Penh, but neither of those are really satisfying.

In Singapore, however, Daniel Goh and his **Smith Street Taps** have you covered. Housed in the sprawling Chinatown Complex Market & Food Centre, Smith Street Taps is an off-shoot of Goh's **Good Beer Company**, Singapore's original craft beer hawker stall. (The Good Beer Company has since moved from the Chinatown Complex and evolved into what Goh describes as "a proper beer bar.") Unusually for Singapore, Smith Street offers ten or more taps of

mainly imported craft beer, from Fourpure Brewing's Indy Lager, which is "(almost) always on tap," to rotating selections of IPAs, stouts, *saisons* and more from as far away as the United States and Sweden.

While speaking to me in 2015 for my book, *The Beer & Food Companion*, Goh said that he opened the Good Beer Company and Smith Street Taps as a way to inject variety into what was then an overly monotone beer culture in Singapore. It worked, and not only does Smith Street now do a brisk trade, Daniel reports that patrons regularly arrive with food in hand, asking staff which beer would best pair with their meal. Even fellow stall owners have sidled over to ask Goh and his business partner Meng Chao what beer styles to partner with the dishes they produce.

While the Chinatown Centre might be somewhat lacking in atmosphere, it more than makes up for it with outstanding food, even boasting a Michelin star in Chef Chan Hon Meng. Coupled with a draught *saison* from the Smith Street, it will likely be the least expensive critically acclaimed meal you're likely ever to come across.

The Chinatown Complex Market and Food Centre

STEPPING INTO GERMANY
AT TAWANDANG

Nobody travels to Thailand for beer. Extraordinary centuries-old temples, yes; the white sand beaches of Phuket, most certainly; and, on a more gastronomic level, definitely the remarkable flavours awaiting foodies in the markets and restaurants of Bangkok. But beer? No. Not even with the wide availability of Singha Lager, a quite credible *märzen*-esque lager masquerading as a mass-market global brand.

But if you find yourself in Thailand anyway, there is one beer destination that should be considered a must for anyone interested in not just good beer, but the cultures that surround its enjoyment: the **Tawandang German Brewery** in Bangkok.

There are now three Tawandang locations in and around the Thai capital, each designed to resemble a king-sized Bavarian beer hall, complete with lengthy rows of communal tables and a massive performance stage at one end. Crowds can grow to as large as 2,000 people at the Ram Indra location, or as relatively modest as the mere 1,000-person capacity of the original

The show never stops at Tawandang.

ADDRESS BOOK

TAWANDANG GERMAN BREWERY
Roma III location: 462/61 Rama 3 Road, Khwaeng Chongnonsi, Khet Yannawa, Bangkok 10120 (two other locations)
tawandang.com

◆

MIKKELLER BANGKOK
26 Ekkamai Soi 10, Yeak 2, Phra Khanong Nuae, Watthana, Bangkok 10110
mikkellerbangkok.com

Tawandang on Rama III, my personal favourite.

For beer, there are quite reasonable interpretations of a *helles*, a *dunkel* and a *hefeweizen*, but in truth the brews are almost beside the point – unless you've been up north drinking Chang for days and feel desperate for something more flavourful, in which case the Tawandang beers will taste like manna from heaven. The real draw here is the experience, from the almost Las Vegas-like countenance of the place to the smiling masses of locals out for a night on the town to the stage show that continues almost non-stop from soon after opening to closing time. To all that, and much more, the beer serves as a tasty, enjoyable accent.

WHILE YOU'RE THERE
For craft beer from Europe and the United States mixed with a handful of Thai brews, drop into **Mikkeller Bangkok**, with 30 taps and almost certainly the best beer selection in town.

KNOCKING BACK *BIA HOÌ*
IN VIETNAM

Let's get one thing straight right off the bat: there is good beer to be found in Vietnam. Jonathan Gharbi, a contributor to *The Pocket Beer Guide/Best Beers* I co-write with Tim Webb, certainly found enough to write his *Beer Guide to Vietnam,* published in 2015, and that was before the impressive Furbrew opened in Hanoi in 2016.

But I'm not going to tell you about Furbrew, or Pasteur Street Brewing or East West Brewing, both promising operations based in Ho Chi Minh City. Instead, my recommendation passes to that Vietnamese staple, *bia hoì.* As generations of backpackers have discovered, the name refers to both a form of fresh, very light beer and the places in which it is enjoyed – or if not necessarily *enjoyed,* then at least *consumed.* Most common in the north of the country, *bia hoì* the beer is brewed from malt, rice and sugar, fermented to about 3% ABV and drunk young, usually poured by gravity from metal kegs for patrons standing or seated on upturned plastic crates around makeshift tables at a *bia hoì,* the bar.

While Gharbi insists that *bia hoìs* of merit do exist, citing one from HABECO in particular, generally speaking, their most positive attributes are that they are: a) refreshing, and b) extremely inexpensive. They also represent both the quintessential Vietnamese experience and a chance to commune with locals, even if such communing does sometimes involve little more than a small handful of shared words and a much larger number of gesticulations.

As for that other beer, the good stuff, it tends toward Czech lager in its styling, Vietnamese brewers having been largely schooled by Czech guest workers, who arrived during communist times and stayed after the dissolution of the Soviet empire. But it's not terribly hard to find Czech-influenced lager almost anywhere in the world; *bia hoì,* on the other hand, is pure Vietnam.

It is suggested that travellers choose their *bia hoì* bars carefully, as some offer better beer and, more importantly, better and safer food than others. An enquiry at the front desk of whichever hotel you are staying in should be enough to steer you in the right direction.

The bia hoì *corner in Hanoi.*

A WEEK OF GOOD BEER
IN MELBOURNE
BY MATT KIRKEGAARD

While every Australian state boasts a "beer week" of some description, the national gathering of the beery tribes is undoubtedly Melbourne's **Good Beer Week**, held early in May each year. Dating back only as far as 2011, the event originally piggybacked off the presence of the country's brewers in town for the Australian International Beer Awards, with a couple of beer-focused events coordinated by enthusiastic volunteers. It has since rapidly expanded to become a professionally run programme bookended by two weekends.

Deliberately taking the name "good" rather than "craft" beer, it runs the gamut of interests, from beer novices through to hard-core aficionados and incorporates beer venues, local breweries and restaurants celebrating beer from all over Melbourne, around the country and across the globe. The formal Australian International Beer Awards presentation dinner is still a major fixture and, though tending toward industry rather than consumer interest, the dinner has upped its game in

Celebrating the Great Australasian Beer SpecTAPular.

recent years. Aspirations lean toward being a showcase of beer and food to match the excellence the awards themselves celebrate.

A city-wide highlight is the Pint of Origin (PoO). Run by leading beer website The Crafty Pint, PoO started out as a series of tap takeovers, each one aiming to showcase a different Australian state – thereby allowing drinkers to sample a cross-section of the country's best beers. As Good Beer Week grew, the PoO did too, adding nomadic brewers, as well as brewers from countries such as New Zealand, the United States

ADDRESS BOOK

GOOD BEER WEEK
goodbeerweek.com.au

Above and top: The Great Australasian Beer SpecTAPular

so perfectly does it lend itself to the task.

GABS celebrates beer, brewing and food all at once in a perfectly executed event that cleverly manages to avoid the boorishness of some beer festivals. Highlights each year are the more than 180 beers brewed specifically for the event, many limited editions or pre-releases, which allow brewers to exercise their creative muscles and test the waters. Call it the lynchpin of a week that highlights all that Australian beer has become, and the potential it yet holds.

and others from northwestern Europe, to the programme.

It would be unfair to describe any event in such a huge week as *the* highlight, but the Great Australasian Beer SpecTAPular, or GABS, is a monolith in the week that could easily stand alone. The venue, the cavernous and World Heritage-listed Royal Exhibition Building, was built in 1880 for an international exhibition and also hosted Australia's first parliament. It could easily have been built to house this festival,

A FLYING PUB CRAWL

Australia is a big place. A really big place, in fact: larger than all but five other nations in the world. In terms of people, however, it's not so big, with only about 24 million inhabitants, which is two-thirds of Canada's relatively sparse population.

That low-resident-to-space ratio means that there is a whole lot of Oz surrounding major cities that is, well, fairly empty. Not in the sense that there is absolutely no one around, mind you; more that towns count their populations in the hundreds rather than the tens or hundreds of thousands.

This makes driving to country pubs from the city centres rather dull and tedious. Helicoptering to those same pubs, on the other hand, is much, much more entertaining. Enter Pterodactyl Helicopters, to my knowledge the only aviation company that offers a helicopter drinking tour, or, as they advertise it, a "country pub crawl by chopper".

Here's how it works. Flights for two to six people depart from one of three locations in the region surrounding Brisbane and then tour to four or five pubs over the course of the day, lunch

ADDRESS BOOK

PTERODACTYL HELICOPTERS
pterodactylhelicopters.com.au

included. Since there are, you know, helicopter flights involved, the pubs visited are selected more for their available space than they are for their beer selection, and the company line is that passengers are limited to one pint per pub. But still, the view from above is spectacular, and even a

single pint per pub makes for five pints over the course of a day.

Of course, pub crawling by air is not cheap, so the cost for a minimum of two people is, as of mid-2017, Australian $940 (£560/US $740), with a $240 (£140/US $190) surcharge if you want to depart from the airfield closest to Brisbane. If you're staying with a friend outside of Brisbane, and said friend has a really big backyard, the company will even fly over to pick you up – for an extra charge, of course. Still, you'll be able to say that you're one of only a handful of people in the world who has gone on a helicopter pub tour, and that is definitely an achievement worth bragging about.

BROWSING BRISBANE
BY MATT KIRKEGAARD

While Brisbane has grown in size and sophistication during the last 20 years, it does still have the tendency common in insecure adolescents to adopt the style of those it admires. In truth, though, the country's third-largest city is at its best when it embraces its own character and charm, especially in the case of food and drink.

Nowhere is this more evident than in craft beer. A relative latecomer to the good beer scene, Brisbane produced the Champion Small Australian Brewery at the 2017 Australian International Beer Awards, as well as boasting the Medium- and Large-scale champions just down the coast.

That Champion Small Brewery is **Green Beacon**, an inner-city brewpub that is well worth a visit. Occupying a reclaimed 1940s warehouse, the venue is sparse and industrial without verging into the craft-beer dive-bar common to many similar brewpubs. The core beer styles are crowd-pleasing standards,

from a *kölsch* interpretation through to a pale ale and an IPA, but they are uniformly excellent. The chance to sample further into the seasonal and limited-release range, plus the brewery's small but awarded barrel-aging programme, cements the need for a visit.

Just a 300-m (984-ft) stroll away in the neighbouring suburb is the eponymous **Newstead Brewing** brewpub. Larger than Green Beacon and with a casual restaurant pushing out pub grub, the regular beers are well made and popular, and the brewery

Green Beacon

also has a vibrant collaboration programme that produces an extensive range of curiosities and esoterica.

Brisbane's climate is moderate, generally staying between 22° and 30°C (71° and 86°F), which has an influence on both beer styles and drinking culture, as well as the architecture of the city's pubs. While, sadly, few of the classic pubs with their wide verandas survive, and fewer are worthy of a visit, the recently renovated **Port Office** in the city centre is an exception. While its beer list blends the country's best independent breweries with beers from the multinationals, the pub really shines as a food venue. Elevating the menu to restaurant-quality fare in a casual setting, Chef Graham Waddell has won plaudits from restaurant reviewers who normally eschew pub dining.

On the fine-dining front, one restaurant to include in any Brisbane visit is **The Catbird Seat**. This intimate, 40-seat bistro offers a clever and contemporary menu that avoids cliché or fads in presenting what is loosely described as modern French, but is really its own, style – yet another example of the city's recently achieved maturity.

Newstead Brewing

A FOURTH AND FINAL
"GREAT"
FESTIVAL

It comes as a surprise to many non-Kiwis that long and narrow New Zealand is a country spread over two islands, with the big names Auckland and Wellington on the North Island and more minor-player cities like Christchurch and Invercargill on the geographically larger South Island. As such, visitors may be inclined to stick to the north and miss out on the charms of the south. At almost any time, this approach is a mistake, but when the **Great Kiwi Beer Festival** is on in late January or February, it's a very large omission indeed.

Given that most international flights land somewhere on the North Island, the first step is to hop on a plane south, which itself is part of the allure. When the weather cooperates, which in New Zealand is most of the time, the scenery flying from Auckland or Wellington to anywhere in the South Island is nothing less than spectacular, and you quickly realize why all the *Lord of the Rings* movies were shot in those gloriously green mountains.

Having arrived in Christchurch, you will be quickly reminded that winter in the northern hemisphere is summer in the southern hemisphere, as well as alerted to the fact that at Great Kiwi Beer Festival time, the city is at the heart of all things New Zealand and beer. Sunscreen applied and well-hydrated, it is festival time!

Held outdoors in idyllic Hagley Park, the festival attracts brewers from all across the country – no small feat in a nation where 2,000 sometimes quite mountainous kilometres (around 1,200 miles) and a stretch of ocean separate its northernmost and southernmost breweries. Organizers supplement this largesse with imported

ADDRESS BOOK

GREAT KIWI BEER FESTIVAL
Hagley Park, Christchurch 8011
greatkiwibeerfestival.co.nz

beers, brewer seminars, chef demonstrations and even a decent amount of local wine for those so inclined.

Yet for all this, perhaps the greatest strength of the GKBF, as it's known, is that it manages to be both mellow and intense. At one end of the park, there are bands on stage and a rock-concert atmosphere for the more boisterous, while a much calmer vibe prevails at the opposite end, where the seminars and demonstrations are held. The combination gives the event an overall ambience equalled by few beer festivals around the globe, and a national importance matched by even fewer.

Above: Enjoying beer... Top: ...and pouring beer at the Great Kiwi Beer Festival.

PUB CRAWLING

IN THE KIWI CAPITAL

ADDRESS BOOK

MALTHOUSE
48 Courtenay Place, Te Aro,
Wellington 6011
themalthouse.co.nz

HASHIGO ZAKE
25 Taranaki Street, Te Aro,
Wellington 6011
hashigozake.co.nz

FORK & BREWER
20A Bond Street, Te Aro,
Wellington 6011
forkandbrewer.co.nz

ROGUE & VAGABOND
18 Garrett Street, Te Aro,
Wellington 6011
rogueandvagabond.co.nz
◆

THE HOP GARDEN
13 Pirie Street, Mount Victoria,
Wellington 6011
thehopgarden.co.nz
◆

LITTLE BEER QUARTER
6 Edward Street, Te Aro,
Wellington 6011
littlebeerquarter.co.nz

While New Zealand boasts the standard one political capital of Wellington, where beer is concerned the country lays claim to two: Nelson, the "Craft Brewing Capital of New Zealand", and Wellington, the "Craft Beer Capital of New Zealand". With all due respect to Nelson, from whence hail the world's great New Zealand hop varieties, Wellington is by far the more interesting. For one thing, you can get around it without having to hop in your car – an obvious plus when on a beer crawl – and secondly, Wellington is simply a lovely city, with an endless parade of theatre, arts, festivals and food to keep you occupied between beer bars.

As for those beer bars, there are a great many. In fact, with almost seven times the population, even northern Auckland can't compare with the impressive Wellington beer scene. Begin at the **Malthouse**, the city's original craft-beer bar and, even after 20 years, still among its finest and most hospitable. You'll recognize immediately that they are serious about beer when you

scan 26 draught taps and find not a single dud (usually, at least); you'll then know this for certain when you note that the bottled selection is divided among six refrigerators, each dialled to the correct temperature for the beer within.

From there, wend your way to beer hotspot **Hashigo Zake**, a Japanese-themed basement bar and restaurant with what is arguably the city's most adventurous beer list. The 11 taps may seem few, but there is little doubt that at least one of the draughts will be something that you a) have never even heard of; and b) will find nowhere else in the city.

From there, much beer still awaits. The **Fork & Brewer**

Fork & Brewer

Hashigo Zake

manages somehow to keep an astounding number of taps filled with its own beers, brewed by ex-Thornbridge brewer Kelly Ryan, and matches them with an equally ambitious kitchen. **The Rogue & Vagabond** leans heavily toward small-scale Kiwi beer on its 15 taps. On the edge of downtown, **The Hop Garden** combines excellent Mediterranean-influenced fare with the best of New Zealand beer and wine. And **Little Beer Quarter** is a semi-hidden oasis with 14 taps, a couple of cask-conditioned ales (usually) and impressive pizzas.

Combined with more than a dozen other respectable beer destinations, Wellington offers more than sufficient proof that it is a very deserving Craft Beer Capital indeed.

Rogue & Vagabond

AFRICAN BEER
WITH A VIEW

While the African continent has much to offer the adventurous traveller, its beer assets are, well, rather less abundant. In fact, they are all but non-existent. Certainly the committed "beer ticker" will see opportunity in the sorghum-heavy Guinness brewed in Nigeria, one of the beer world's earliest "white whales" as such rare and sought-after brews have come to be known. But the truth is that, once in Nigeria, that beer is fairly abundant and, frankly, not even all that great.

Having been so disappointed, the committed beer traveller might then head to Kenya, where Nairobi offers two possibilities in the form of Sierra and Big Five, each breweries with more potential than current interest, or Addis Ababa in Ethiopia and the more-than-just-competent beers of the Beer Garden Inn. Then you might point south, where everyone says resides the best hope for African craft beer. If lucky, our intrepid explorer will find a way to the Spice Route in Paarl, South Africa, just outside of Cape Town, and

there he or she will find what is perhaps the continent's finest beer experience.

For lack of a better word, the Spice Route is a farm on which numerous businesses operate, all with an exquisite view of the surrounding mountains. There is a winery, a glass studio, a chocolatier, a distillery, several fine restaurants, and there is the Cape Brewing Company (CBC).

Headed by a former brewer for the Munich-based brewing company Paulaner, Cape Brewing is a leader in the Western Cape craft-beer market, one of the largest and most successful small breweries in South Africa and almost certainly the one in the most idyllic location. With a brewmaster whose first job was in a Bavarian brewery, it's hardly surprising that CBC's strength is in German-style lagers and wheat beers, including the Pilsner, estimated by South African beer writer Lucy Corne to be the country's finest. In a concession to modern times, there is also an IPA, of course, but one seasoned with the recently cultivated Mandarina Bavaria hop from Germany.

The brewery's tasting room is exactly that – for tasting rather than drinking – but that's of little

Cooling shade at the Spice Route.

Spectacular views from the Spice Route.

ADDRESS BOOK

**CAPE BREWING COMPANY/
SPICE ROUTE**
*Suid Agter Paarl Road,
Suider Paarl 7624
capebrewing.co.za
spiceroute.co.za*

concern when there are so many excellent restaurant and casual-dining options nearby, from the Barley & Biltong Emporium, a "beer garden with a Cape twist" that features burgers and CBC beers, to Chef Bertus Basson's eponymous restaurant.

More great South African and African beer destinations are sure to follow in due course. But for now, only the most discourteous visitor would complain after a day spent at Spice Route, admiring the views and enjoying the technically and flavourfully impressive beers of the Cape Brewing Company.

GLOSSARY

A

ABV – Alcohol by volume. The volume of alcohol relative to the total volume of a beverage.

ALE – Beer resulting from warm fermentation by yeast of the family *Saccharomyces cerevisiae*. Sometimes referred to as top-fermented or warm-fermented.

ALTBIER – A style of warm-fermented, cold-conditioned beer associated with the German city of Düsseldorf.

B

BARLEY WINE – Term used historically to denote the strongest beer in a brewer's portfolio, often of low carbonation or even "flat", with the strength of a light wine. Nowadays it is more often a specific style of strong ale, hoppier in the American interpretation.

BERLINER WEISSE – Low strength, tart style of wheat beer originating from Berlin, but now frequently brewed elsewhere.

BIÈRE DE GARDE – Literally "beer for keeping", this refers to a strong French ale style traditionally brewed in the spring for storage over the non-brewing summer months.

BITTER – Today the standard ale of British pubs, often fashioned as Best Bitter. Pale, mildly to moderately hopped and in its modern incarnation 3.5–4.5% ABV.

BOCK - Strong, robust and malty-tasting German lager with an average ABV of 5.5–7.5%.

BOTTLE SHOP – Common term used to denote a shop that sells beer, wine and/or spirits.

BRETTANOMYCES – Literally "British fungus", a type of wild (naturally occurring) yeast that can have both good and bad influences on beer fermentation and flavour. Also known simply as "Brett".

C

CAMRA – The Campaign for Real Ale. Organization founded in the UK in 1971 for the preservation of traditional cask-conditioned ales.

CIDER – Alcoholic beverage made from fermented apple juice and varying widely in strength and sweetness. In the United States, commonly "hard cider".

D

DOPPELBOCK – A stronger version of a *bock*, with an average ABV of 6.5–9%.

DUNKEL – Dark lager of a style once native to Munich and the surrounding area. Sometimes referred to as *Münchner*.

E

EISBOCK – A very strong, *bock*-style beer that is produced by freezing and removing some of the water used in brewing, thereby concentrating the resulting beer's flavour, body and alcohol content.

F

FOEDER – A large wooden cask used by breweries to condition and age beers, typically of the sort classed as mixed fermentation or sometimes "sour" beers.

FRAMBOISE – Type of Belgian lambic beer that is fermented with raspberries.

G

GUEUZE (OR GEUZE) – Type of Belgian lambic beer made by blending lambics of different ages (young and old), then bottling for a second fermentation. When designated *oud(e)* or *vieille* it must contain 100 percent lambic beer only.

GRODZISKIE – Traditional and once extinct style of Polish beer made using oak-smoked wheat malt.

H

HELLES – Pale lager style originally associated with Munich and the surrounding areas. Sometimes referred to as *Münchner helles*.

I

IPA (INDIA PALE ALE) – Style of pale ale that derives its name from its popularity in India during the days of the Raj. Originally native to England, it is now recognised in American (very hoppy and moderately strong) and British (less assertively hopped and lighter) versions, plus numerous derivatives such as Double IPA (stronger and hoppier), Session IPA (lower strength) and Black IPA (dark brown or black without excessive roasted character).

K

KAIMISKA – Rustic form of full-bodied, tangy, fruity Lithuanian ale, traditionally brewed at a farmhouse.

KÖLSCH – A style of light blond, warm-fermented and cold-conditioned beer, confined by legislation in the European Union to the German city of Cologne (Köln) and its immediate area, but still imitated elsewhere.

KRIEK – Belgian lambic beer that is fermented with sour cherries.

L

LAGER – Beer resulting from cool fermentation by yeast of the *Saccharomyces pastorianus* family, traditionally afforded a long cold conditioning or maturing period. Sometimes referred to as bottom-fermented or cool-fermented.

LAMBIC – Collective name for the family of beers fermented by the action of wild yeast and also the name given to the unblended draught form of such beers.

M

MÄRZEN – Moderately strong style of German lager historically brewed in the month of March for cellaring and consumption during the non-brewing summer season. Widely associated with autumn festivals, such as Munich's Oktoberfest.

MILD – Traditional British

term originally used to describe immature beer but now used as a style term denoting ales light in alcohol, usually dark in colour and predominantly malty.

P

PASTEURIZATION – A means of cleansing microorganisms from beer (or other consumables) by applying heat for a brief period of time, stopping short of sterilization.

PILSNER – Pale lager first brewed in the Bohemian, now Czech, city of Plzen (Pilsen), rendered meaningless as a style by the ruling of a Munich court in 1899 to allow its use for lesser beers.

PORTER – A moderately bitter, deep brown or black style of ale originating in London in the eighteenth century. In modern terms, similar to stout. In the US, sometimes modified as Robust Porter to refer to a beer of higher strength and bitterness.

R

RAUCHBIER – German style of lager made using a portion of malts that have been smoked over wood, typical of Bamberg and the surrounding area.

REINHEITSGEBOT – The Bavarian beer purity law of 1516, adopted across the whole of Germany in 1919 but ruled a restriction of trade by the European Union in 1988.

S

SAHTI – Traditional Finnish style of beer brewed from barley and rye, fermented with bread yeast and filtered through juniper branches.

SCHWARZBIER – Type of black hued, dominantly malty lager once typical of eastern Germany.

STANGE – Traditional tall, cylindrical glass with thin walls, used for drinking *kölsch* beers.

STOUT – A family of black or near-black ales originally derived from porter, including oatmeal, milk, oyster, Irish, dry, smoked, sweet, export, Imperial and others, ranging widely in strength, degree of sweetness and hoppiness, but always featuring some measure of roasty character.

T

TIED HOUSE – A pub or bar that is "tied" to a brewery or pub company, meaning that it is required to sell the beer made by that company. A free house, by contrast, can sell any beer its proprietors wish to sell.

TRIPEL – The strongest type of beer produced by monastic breweries and their imitators, originally dark and made with three times the malt used in standard beer, but nowadays usually golden, after Westmalle Tripel from the Belgian Trappist abbey of that name, near Antwerp.

W

WEIZENBIER (ALSO WEISSBIER OR HEFEWEIZEN) – Denoting a style of wheat beer typical to southern Germany, it contains a large proportion of malted wheat and produces banana and clove aromas during fermentation with yeast. When filtered, generally referred to as Kristallweizen or Kristallklar Weissbier.

WHITE BEER (ALSO WIT OR BIÈRE BLANCHE) – A style of beer typical to Belgium, made with barley malt and unmalted wheat, nowadays usually spiced with dried orange peel and coriander, plus sometimes other spices, too.

INDEX

ACKNOWLEDGEMENTS

After more than 27 years of travelling for beer, the list of individuals I need to thank could easily consume an entire chapter of this book, so I must begin by acknowledging all those who will by necessity go unnamed here. To everyone with whom I have travelled, whose local knowledge I have mined for information, and who have been kind enough to share their time with me over a pint or a meal somewhere around the world, I thank you most sincerely.

More specific thanks go out to the global community of beer writers and bloggers who have helped me out in so many ways, furthering my research even while sacrificing their own work time, beginning with my esteemed colleague and frequent co-author, Tim Webb, and continuing to others including, but by no means limited to, Max Bahnson, Jay Brooks, Pete Brown, Lew Bryson, Lauren Clark, Lorenzo Dabove, John Duffy, Stan Hieronymus, Matt Kirkegaard, Maurizio Maestrelli, Neil Miller, Des de Moor, Lisa Morrison, Josh Oakes, Luc De Raedemaeker, Evan Rail, Tim Skelton, Joe Stange, Adrian Tierney-Jones, Michelle Wang, Joe Wiebe and Kathia Zanatta.

For recognizing the potential of this and other books I have authored or co-authored, I would like to thank the best publisher with whom it has ever been my privilege to work, Denise Bates, as well as others at Octopus including Matthew Grindon, Liz Hermann, Ella Parsons and Andrew Welham. For being such a terrific agent, I would like also to extend my heartfelt thanks to Clare Pelino.

My family and my friends are my strength, and deepest gratitude to you all for being there when I needed you. And finally, but most importantly, an endless thank you to my wonderful wife and fellow travel addict, Maggie.

PICTURE CREDITS